The Corporate Contributions Function

by Kathryn Troy

A Research Report from The Conference Board

Contents

Page

WHY THIS REPORT vii

1. OVERVIEW 1
   Methodology... 1
   Definitions and Limitations..................................... 2
   Highlights of Survey Findings 3
   Organization of the Contributions Function 3
   Job Titles and Responsibilities................................. 3
   The Process... 3
   Planning, Budgeting, People and Communications 3

2. STRUCTURE, PHILOSOPHY AND GOVERNANCE 5
   Budget Size and Contributions Structure......................... 5
   Contributions Structure and Philosophy: Implications for the Future 6
   Two Approaches: Centralized and Decentralized 6
   Future Directions... 7
   The Governance of Corporate Contributions Programs 7
   Foundation and Direct Mechanisms................................ 7
   Decision Making and Governance in a Direct-Giving Program....... 8
   The Contributions Committee 8
   Governance in Foundation Boards................................. 9
   The Board of Trustees... 9

3. RESPONSIBILITIES OF THE CORPORATE CONTRIBUTIONS OFFICER 13
   An Overview: Reporting Relationships and Staffing Patterns 13
   Direct-Giving Programs... 13
   Company Foundations 14
   In-Depth Profiles 16
   Corporate Vice Presidents as Contributions Officers 16
   Others with Corporate Titles and Contributions Responsibilities 20
   Contributions Specialists...................................... 20
   Executives in Direct-Giving Programs 20
   Staff in Direct-Giving Programs................................ 21
   Company Foundation Programs 21
   Related Responsibilities....................................... 22

4. HOW THE CONTRIBUTIONS PROCESS WORKS 23
   Planning... 23
   Budgeting 24
   Setting Budget Guidelines 24

　　　　　Determining a Level for Uncommitted Funds 25
　　　　　Headquarters and Field Allocations. 25
　　　　　Approval Authority. 27
　　　　　Number and Size of Grants 29
　　　　　Supplements to Contributions 31
　　　　Carrying Out the Contributions Program 32
　　　　　Interaction with Top Corporate Executives 32
　　　　　　Influence on Program Content and Grant Size. 33
　　　　　Interaction with Related Corporate Departments. 33
　　　　　　Use of Other Departments for Contributions-Related Matters 34
　　Communications. 35
　　　　Industry Patterns. 35
　　　　Shareholders 37

APPENDIX: JOB RESPONSIBILITY PROFILE. 38

APPENDIX TABLES
A-1. Contributions Job Responsibility Profile 38
A-2. Company Foundation Presidents and Vice Presidents 39
A-3. Department Administering United Way Campaign. 39
A-4. Department Administering Matching Gifts. 39

Tables

1. Corporate Giving Mechanisms 8
2. Organizational Location of Direct Corporate Giving Program 8
3. The Corporate Contributions Committee. 9
4. Number of Members on Corporate Contributions Committee 9
5. Membership of Contributions Committees and Foundation Boards 10
6. Number of Members on Foundation Boards. 10
7. Number of Members on Foundation Boards. 11
8. Members of Foundation Boards Who Are Also Corporate Directors 12
9. Outside Directors of Company Foundation 12
10. Total Staff Size in Foundation and Direct-Giving Programs. 13
11. Median Number of Staff in Direct-Giving Programs. 14
12. Reporting Relationships of Top Executives Responsible for
　　Direct-Giving Program 14
13. Disciplines or Areas of Specialization among Professional Staff. 15
14. Median Number of Staff in Foundation Programs 15
15. Highest Ranking Foundation Officials Who Also Hold Corporate Titles 15
16. Contributions Staff Size. 16
17. Corporate Strategic Planning and Contributions Planning 23
18. Corporate Strategic Planning and Contributions Planning 24
19. Factors Considered in Setting Size of Total Contributions Budget 24
20. Basis for Setting Budget Target. 26
21. Basis for Setting Budget Target Using Pretax Net Income. 26
22. Percentage of Budget Left Uncommitted 26
23. Headquarters Role in Field Decision Making 27
24. Percentage of Budget Spent by Headquarters and Field Locations 27
25. Percentage of Budget Spent by Headquarters and Field Locations 28
26. Percentage of Budget Spent by Headquarters and Field Locations 28
27. Individuals and Groups Having Approval Authority 29

28. Approval Authority in Direct-Giving Programs 29
29. Approval Authority in Foundation Programs....................... 29
30. Approval Authority for Budgeted Items 30
31. Approval Authority for Contingency Items 30
32. Grant Size for Direct-Giving Programs............................ 30
33. Grant Size for Company Foundations 30
34. Supplements to Charitable Contributions.......................... 32
35. Interaction with Top Management by Person Responsible for
    Contributions Program...................................... 32
36. Interaction with Top Management by Person Responsible for
    Contributions Program...................................... 33
37. Interaction with Top Management by Person Responsible for
    Contributions Program...................................... 33
38. Influence of Corporate Executives and Governing Groups
    on Program Content 34
39. Influence of Corporate Executives and Governing Groups on Size of Grants . 34
40. Frequency of Interaction between Contributions Personnel
    and other Departments 35
41. Use of Other Corporate Departments for Contributions-Related Tasks 35
42. Use of Other Departments and Consultants for Contributions-Related Tasks. 36
43. Communications Practices in Contributions Programs................. 36
44. Communications Practices in Contributions Programs................. 36
45. Companies Reporting Contributions in Annual Report 37

Charts

1. Contributions Practitioners: Salary Level, Reporting Relationship
   and Time Spent on Contributions 18
2. Change in Size of Grants over the Last Three Years 31
3. Change in Number of Grants over the Last Three Years 31

Acknowledgments

Special thanks are due to the following Conference Board colleagues: *Questionnaire Coding and Editing,* Selma Mackler, Staff Assistant, Public Affairs Research Division; *Data Processing,* Merry Law, Survey Research Associate, Survey Research Center; *Manuscript Editing,* Lillian W. Kay, Manager, Editorial Services Department and Paul Smolenski, Editorial Associate; *Charting,* Chuck N. Tow, Lead Chartist, and Laura Gross, Senior Chartist, Charting Department; *Typesetting,* Linda Saladino, Office Services Department; *Production,* Alice Miller, Production Specialist, Graphics and Production Department.

Why This Report

Public opinion and public policy, as exemplified by the Administration's New Federalism, are placing increased emphasis on the private business sector's participation in the voluntary sector. Since 1936, when corporations were first allowed to claim a charitable deduction on their federal income tax returns, management and boards of directors have become highly aware of the desirability of such social involvement. The amounts contributed annually have increased over the period from $30 million to an estimated $2.7 billion in 1980.

As budgets for corporate philanthropy grow, it is inevitable that more attention will be focused on how this function is managed. The Conference Board has been tracking the growth of corporate contributions through company foundations and direct-giving programs since 1945. We believe it is now important to consider the provisions being made for administering these funds and to seek relationships between contributions budgets and organization.

JAMES T. MILLS
President

Chapter 1
Overview

OBSERVERS of U.S. society from de Tocqueville onward have noted its unique tradition of voluntarism. Traditionally, individual citizens have been the major source of time and dollars for what at various times has been dubbed the third, or voluntary, sector of U.S. society—more than 300,000 nonprofit agencies supplying services in health, welfare, education, culture, community services, and the like. While individuals continue to be the major source of support for nonprofit agencies, corporations have become an increasingly visible force. In 1936, the first year that corporations were allowed to claim a charitable deduction on their federal tax return, total contributions were $30 million; in 1980, they are estimated to be $2.7 billion.[1]

In the years since the New Deal, the Federal Government also became an increasingly important source of support for social programs. But since the 1970's, some observers have been suggesting that the Federal Government has overextended itself, contributing to slowing economic growth.

The 1980 presidential election and the advent of the Reagan Administration and the "new federalism" appear to have brought an end to the period of Federal Government expansion in the area of social programs. With the recent appointment (December, 1981) of a presidential task force, new emphasis has been placed on "private-sector initiatives" in the social arena. Individuals, corporations and foundations are being asked to mobilize themselves to help fill the gap that is expected to result from cutbacks in federal support. Within this new climate of emphasis on private-sector initiatives, this report focuses on *corporate* philanthropic programs. The objectives of the study were to explore and describe the job responsibilities of corporate contributions officers and the organization of the corporate contributions function at the headquarters locations of major U.S. corporations.

Methodology

The sample selected for this study was the 1000 largest manufacturing firms listed by *Fortune* for 1980, as well as the 50 largest nonmanufacturing firms in each of six areas: banking, life insurance, financial services, retailing, transportation and utilities. The nonmanufacturing sample of 300 companies was supplemented with a mailing to 150 firms just below the size of those on the *Fortune* list.

In June, 1980, two questionnaires and a covering letter were mailed to the contributions officer in each corporation in the sample, with a request that the material be returned by July 25, 1980. The first questionnaire was a profile of the contributions officer, requesting information on background, career path, job responsibilities and compensation. The covering letter requested that one response be returned for each member of the professional staff. To guarantee confidentiality, respondents were instructed to return the questionnaires in a plain envelope.

The senior person responsible for contributions was asked to complete the second questionnaire, which was a profile of the contributions function. This questionnaire required company identification, with a guarantee of confidentiality. Individual profiles were returned by 524 professionals; profiles of the function were returned by 435 companies. The company responses were distributed as follows:

Manufacturing:

Top 500 on *Fortune* list:	202 Companies
Second 500 on *Fortune* list:	93 Companies

Nonmanufacturing:

Fortune 300 list:	97 Companies
Supplemental mailing (150):	43 Companies
Total:	435 Companies

---

[1] Individuals account for almost 90 percent of total philanthropy in the United States. On the average, corporate giving has been about 5 percent of the total throughout the last 25 years. Foundation giving (other than through corporate foundations) has dropped from 9 to 5 percent of the total over the past decade. (Inflation and other factors have eroded foundation assets.) In this climate, nonprofit agencies have turned to corporations for increased support. Information on total philanthropy can be found in *Giving USA*. American Association of Fund Raising Counsel, Inc., New York, Annual.

On August 1, 1980, a brief follow-up questionnaire was sent to the 925 companies in the original sample that did not respond, asking that they indicate the reason for not responding. This questionnaire drew replies from 128 companies (see box).

Definitions and Limitations

Corporate contributions programs are administered either directly through the corporation or indirectly through a company foundation (some companies use both mechanisms). Throughout this study, those administered through the corporation are referred to as *direct-giving* programs; those administered through a company foundation are designated *foundation* programs.

Several of the tables in this report and much of the discussion in Chapter 3 relate to the job titles of those administering contributions programs. Three basic classifications have been used:

Corporate titles refer to those whose titles indicate that their main function is something other than contributions (e.g., vice president, administration, corporate secretary, assistant to the president).

Contributions titles refer to those whose titles indicate that they have responsibility in a direct-giving program (e.g., manager of corporate contributions, corporate contributions analyst).

Foundation titles refer to those whose titles indicate that their chief responsibility is in a company foundation (e.g., vice president, foundation program officer).

Within each group, those with titles such as president or vice president are separated from those who had executive and staff titles.

Budget size is an indicator used frequently in analyzing data throughout this report. In consulting the tables that group companies by budget size, it is important to note that the data for companies having both foundation and direct-giving programs reflect the total contributions budget. For comparability, one must use the sum of foundation and direct-giving program budgets.

How much can be generalized from the data in this study, given the size and constitution of the sample? In the past, analysis of responses to the Board's Annual Survey of Corporate Contributions had suggested that formally structured and professionally staffed programs were most likely to exist among the larger, *Fortune*-size companies, as well as among those large- and medium-sized nonmanufacturing companies that had visibility in their communities (e.g., banks, utilities, retailers, insurance companies). The data collected in this survey reinforce that conclusion.

The number of *Fortune*-size companies with a structured contributions program, that also employ a staff

Reasons for Not Responding to Contributions Function Survey

	Number of Companies
Contributions function has an informal structure that does not fit into questionnaire format	89
Corporation has policy against responding to questionnaires	11
Corporation does not have a contributions function	9
Responding to questionnaire was too time-consuming	7
Corporation was recently merged into another corporation; parent company administers contributions	5
Contributions function is in process of reorganization	4
Other	15
Total	140[a]

[a]Includes 12 telephoned responses.

person with a title specifically related to contributions (whether in a foundation or a direct-giving program), is probably in the range of three to four hundred.[2] If this is the case, the more than 200 companies in this survey that indicate they have a structured, professionally staffed program constitute about half of the total universe for such programs. For this group, counts of 30 or 40 responses shown on some of the tables in this report, while small in absolute terms, are significant in relative terms and probably represent at least 10 percent of the available cases.

The other half of the 435 company responses to this survey represent the larger universe of companies on the *Fortune* list. Some of these companies (roughly 140 to 150) have a structured or semistructured program and a staff member who devotes in the range of one-quarter to one-half time to contributions. There are probably no more than 500 companies on the *Fortune* list that resemble this group, so that these respondents represent at least 20 percent of that universe. Others among the respondents (roughly 60 to 70 companies), have a program which more closely resembles the "informally structured" programs claimed by many of those answer-

---

[2]Indicators of a structured program include a written policy statement, a contributions plan and budget, and a board or committee system.

ing the follow-up questionnaire. This group represents about 12 to 15 percent of the remaining 400 to 500 *Fortune*-size companies, primarily those near the lower end of the list.

Generally speaking, the larger a company's contributions budget, and the more specifically related the job title is to contributions, the greater the likelihood that the results of this study are applicable. However, those in the middle group described above should also be able to generalize from the data with a moderately high level of confidence. Those with an informally structured program will find the data least applicable in an immediate sense, but should derive benefit if they choose to use them to structure their program in the future.

Highlights of Survey Findings

Organization of the Contributions Function

- A direct corporate-giving program was the only contributions mechanism for over half of the respondents, while almost a third (30 percent) combined the direct-giving mechanism with a company foundation. Only 18 percent of the companies used a foundation as the sole giving mechanism.
- In most cases (70 percent), direct-giving programs are governed by a contributions committee. These are usually made up of members of the management of the corporation, with a median of five members. Foundation boards have a median of six members, and in 80 percent of the cases this includes members of the corporate board. Outsiders serve on a third of the foundation boards, while this is true of only 7 percent of the contributions committees. Both committees and boards usually meet on a quarterly basis.
- In about 80 percent of the cases, committees and boards have a primary role in budget review and approval. Within this group, approvals are made either on a line-by-line basis or on totals by major budget category.
- About 70 percent of those with direct-giving programs and 80 percent of those with foundations indicate that they have a staff. Staff sizes are generally small: The median count is two to three people, consisting of a general administrator, a specialist (program officer or analyst), and a secretary or clerk. Not all staff members work full time.

Job Titles and Responsibilities

- Among foundation personnel, the highest ranking professional is a foundation president or vice president in about half the cases; an executive director in 20 percent; and a secretary or treasurer in about 13 percent. The rest are dispersed among different functions. In direct-giving programs, the highest ranking person has a contributions-related title in only about half the cases—usually director or manager. In the other half, someone with a corporate title (usually a vice president) is the highest ranking individual.
- The CEO appears to have a great deal of influence on contributions. Those responsible for contributions report meeting with their CEO's on at least a monthly basis and rate the CEO's influence on program content and grant size as about a four on a five-point scale. In companies with small contributions budgets, the CEO sometimes functions as the contributions officer and makes decisions alone. As budgets grow, contributions committees take over part of the decision making in direct-giving programs. Those with foundations appear to increase the *size* of their boards.
- The most basic responsibilities of the contributions officer are screening requests, executing grant approval, and handling related correspondence, payment procedures, and record keeping. As budgets grow, budget preparation and administration, development of policy and procedures, and coordination of the work of the contributions committee and foundation board are added responsibilities.
- As time and staffing permit, those in fully professionalized functions develop a long-range contributions plan, and designate a part of their budget for development of projects which they investigate and initiate. They develop a process for using the expertise of other corporate personnel in planning, proposal screening, and evaluation, and institute a program for communicating the contributions story inside and outside the corporation.

The Process

Planning, Budgeting, People and Communications

- A written policy statement is usually developed at the end point of the contributions planning process. However, although 70 percent of the companies have a policy statement, a smaller proportion say that they have developed a long-range contributions plan. About 60 percent of the foundations and a third of those with direct-giving programs had done some long-range planning. It is possible that the others developed policy statements at the end of a one-time-only planning process.
- All but a few of the companies have a contributions budget and a system for grant authorization. The median approval authority for the CEO ranges from $10,000 in direct-giving programs to $5,000 in foundation programs. At the low end of the scale, direct-giving programs allow local managers a median approval of $500. Local managers rarely have approval authority in foundation programs; within that mechanism, the median for the lowest approval level is $1,250 for program officers.

- There is some involvement by field locations in most contributions programs, although this is likely to be greater in direct-giving programs than in foundation programs. Overall, headquarters operations have authority over 80 percent of the total budget; the field has authority over the remaining 20 percent. However, this may vary by industry—retailers are more likely to decentralize their program and give the field greater authority; banks, insurance companies, and utilities are more likely to focus on their headquarters and surrounding communities. To coordinate work at field locations, at least half of the companies surveyed have developed a set of written guidelines.

- In addition to support from field locations, contributions officers frequently use colleagues in public affairs, community relations, and personnel to help in screening requests, program planning, and monitoring and evaluation of grants. The larger the contributions budget, the greater the likelihood that other departments in the corporation will be tapped to lend their expertise for contributions tasks. A small number of companies (about 25) also use outside consultants.

- Almost half of the companies in the survey communicate with their employees about contributions, while about a quarter keeps the public informed through press releases or a public report of their contributions.

Chapter 2
Structure, Philosophy and Governance

DECISIONS about building new plants, issuing additional stock, investing in new product lines, withdrawing from a shrinking market, or realigning the investment portfolio are a familiar and necessary part of life in most major U.S. corporations. Somewhere, in many of these corporations, executives also make decisions about another set of issues. They ask such questions as:

- How can we ensure that the communities in which we operate provide our employees with adequate health care, human-service support, housing and recreation?
- What can we do to safeguard quality and encourage improvement in our educational system and in artistic and cultural endeavors?
- How can we best attract talented employees to our organization and to our operating communities?

Some business observers may argue that corporate decisions in the "community" or "social sphere" are an improper, or at least an unorthodox, interpretation of the corporate role. Others may argue that they are as essential to the short- and long-term prosperity and survival of the corporation as are its more specifically defined economic decisions. Most would agree that the results of decisions about social or community investments are more difficult to measure.

Currently, at least 83 percent of large U.S. corporations (those with assets of $100 million or more) are making decisions about social needs in the communities in which they operate. They do so when they make the donations which they deduct as charitable contributions on their federal income tax returns.[1] Cash contributions by U.S. corporations increased from $797 million to $2.7 billion between 1970 and 1980. Each year, a growing number of corporations issue some kind of public report about cash contributions and other corporate activities that benefit society. In the Spring of 1981, the Business Roundtable, a forum comprised of top executives from major U.S. corporations, stated this position:

"All business entities should recognize philanthropy both as good business and as an obligation if they are to be considered responsible corporate citizens of the national and local communities in which they operate."[2]

In its efforts to cut government spending and decentralize decision making on social programs to the state and local level, the Reagan Administration has suggested that corporations might be one of several private-sector sources that would pitch in to "fill the gap" in funding nonprofit organizations. There have been conflicting reports about how large this gap will be. A study commissioned by the Independent Sector, an umbrella organization that represents the interests of the voluntary sector, estimates that $25.5 billion that would have been allocated to nonprofit organizations for fiscal years 1982 to 1984 has been eliminated from the federal budget.[3] Since total corporate philanthropy for 1980 was $2.7 billion, it seems unlikely that corporations alone can fill the void. However, whether the increased emphasis on the role of corporate philanthropy is transitory or a portent of change remains an open question. Focusing upon budget size as a key factor, this chapter examines contributions structure and philosophy in an evolutionary context.

Budget Size and Contributions Structure

Historically, the development of corporate contributions and its placement in the corporate structure appear

---

[1] Under the Economic Recovery Tax Act of 1981, corporations will be allowed to take deductions of up to 10 percent of their taxable income as charitable contributions on their federal income tax return. The previous limit of 5 percent had been in effect since 1936. Analysis of Internal Revenue Service data from the 1977 year, as yet unpublished, indicates that 65 percent of the 1.4 million corporations that had a positive income in that year did not make charitable contributions. However, these 918,881 companies had only 15 percent of the assets and income reported in that year. The other 35 percent of the companies did make contributions. They accounted for 85 percent of the assets and income reported.

[2] The Business Roundtable Position on Corporate Philanthropy. The Business Roundtable, March 26, 1981.

[3] Lester M. Salamon and Alan J. Abramson, *The Federal Government and the Nonprofit Sector: Implications of the Reagan Budget Proposals.* Washington, D.C.: The Urban Institute, 1981.

to be more a function of executive personality and circumstance (i.e., retirement, realignment of responsibilities) than of organizational planning. While its history makes it more idiosyncratic than predictable, some general patterns can be discerned that correspond roughly to the growth in the contributions budget.

Programs often begin with very small budgets, reflect the community interests of the chief executive officers, and are administered by them as an after-hours activity. However, as companies expand this activity and budgets grow from a few thousand dollars to $100,000—and then to $300,000 or $400,000—administrative tasks increase, proposal screening becomes more time-consuming, paperwork becomes heavier and, eventually, one or two other employees may become involved, spending less than a quarter of their time on the function. When budgets pass the $500,000 mark, half-time attention may be required; by the $1 million mark, a full-time obligation is frequently involved. Although the reporting relationships frequently remain at a high level (vice president or above), the title of the person with daily contributions responsibility moves from CEO to vice president to director or manager and, sometimes, to a staff title (such as analyst or coordinator).

Formal structures for contributions become more complex. Basically, corporations may choose to make charitable contributions directly to eligible nonprofit organizations, or they may choose to establish a company foundation to which they give funds. The company foundation, in turn, makes contributions to eligible nonprofit groups. As the budget grows, governance of the direct-giving program may be turned over to a contributions committee; a new company foundation may be established; or the board of the existing foundation may be expanded to include more than the few top company officers who had been serving on it. Plans and budgets are developed for annual review by these governing bodies; a statement of contributions policy may be written and guidelines for the field developed. A formal structure of approval limits for grants by headquarters and field locations may evolve.

A third of the companies participating in this survey had a contributions officer who spent more than half time on the function and had established a formal contributions structure. A quarter had a structure, but did not yet have a person working more than half time on the function. The remaining 42 percent were in the process of evolution, building some elements of the structure, but not yet ready for others. For the most part, the staffs were spending less than a quarter of their time on philanthropy.

Contributions Structure and Philosophy: Implications for the Future

Because of the many variations within and among the companies responding to this survey, it has not always been possible to find a method of analysis that yields clear-cut patterns. The company foundation as against the direct corporate giving structure is a good example of the problem. Both large and small companies have foundations; many companies have both foundation and direct corporate-giving programs. Some direct-giving programs appear to be run like company foundations, and vice versa. However, it is possible to make two basic statements about the general characteristics of the direct-giving and foundation programs represented in this study:

• Overall, company foundations appear to centralize approval authority and decision making about grants within the foundation structure; direct-giving programs are more likely to disperse approvals throughout the corporation; decisions on grants below a set limit may also be decentralized. Among the reasons sometimes given for having a company foundation are the increased visibility of the philanthropic program that emanates from a foundation with the company name and the greater insulation of top executives from pressure to commit to grants. Probably the most concrete rationale offered is that of companies that are in cyclical industries. The foundation mechanism allows them to set aside reserve funds in profitable years for use in years of level or decreased profitability.

• The governing board in foundations is composed of high-level corporate executives (often members of the corporate board of directors) and may also include influential people from outside the corporation. Contributions committees are usually management committees, and may include representatives from field locations and from positions below the middle-management level. Few committees have members from outside the corporation (see pages 7 and 8).

Two Approaches: Centralized and Decentralized

Such structural elements sometimes reflect different philosophies of corporate giving. Given its centralized approval system and the nature of its governing board, the foundation structure may be more "elitist" (this is not meant as a pejorative term), while the direct-giving structure—when accompanied by decentralization of approvals and decision making—may be more "democratic." While neither of these philosophies is inherent in these structures, an appreciation of them may be important to those companies developing a new program or reappraising an existing one.

One of the reasons corporations have moved toward permanent staffing for corporate contributions has been the need to develop in-house expertise in grant making. Very often, development of such expertise is accompanied by:

• A more concentrated effort to gather data about

society's needs, including polling of such experts as the outsiders who serve on foundation boards.

- Development of a less parochial (in terms of short-term corporate interests) but at the same time a more focused giving program (e.g., electing to emphasize a few priority areas for giving).
- A search for greater grant impact, sometimes through making fewer, but larger, better targeted grants.

Some of these developments might be interpreted as a movement toward elitism; however, as strategies they do not differ significantly from those employed in other areas of business. Effectiveness and efficiency are corporate watchwords.

Following an alternate line of reasoning, it can be argued that the interests of a corporate philanthropy program *should* be parochial, in the sense that it should address immediate needs in headquarters and field locations, and should be democratic in allowing all corporate locations a share of the budget and a say in how it is dispensed. This approach requires less centralized decision making, and may be a less time-consuming method for delivering contributions to a large number of organizations; those "on the scene" determine what the needs are. More companies continue to encourage employee involvement in contributions through matching-gift programs, and there have been some recent suggestions that shareholders be given a say in how allocations are made. However, the more democratic approach does raise questions about scattered resources and lessened impact.

Future Directions

Those companies that have small programs, but can foresee the time when their budgets will pass $500,000 and then $1 million, will need to ask themselves how these alternate models fit into their own corporate style of decision making.

Over the next few years, as the current federal program of block grants is enacted and the effects on local communities are felt, it seems probable that corporations will be faced with problems of a "parochial" nature in their headquarters and plant communities. It is likely that some piece of the contributions program will have to be decentralized. However, if the grant-making professionalism corporations develop at their headquarters is not shared with the field, the dollars allocated to contributions might be invested with less than maximum return. Headquarters contributions staffs are usually small, and participants in this survey indicate that training field personnel is infrequently a part of their job. One of the challenges lying ahead for those corporations that are concerned about the effectiveness of their contributions and other social investments is to develop a practical system for melding grant-making professionalism with local responsiveness.[4]

The Governance of Corporate Contributions Programs

While the chief executive officer is usually influential in making decisions on contributions, this responsibility is often shared with others in the top management circle. Data from this study show that those with the rank of vice president and above are the most frequent participants in contributions committees and foundation boards. However, these governing groups are not selected exclusively from top management "insiders"; first- and second-line managers and staff people do have representation on some contributions committees, and about a third of the foundation boards include representatives from outside the corporation.

Foundation and Direct Mechanisms

A company foundation was the only mechanism for 77 of the companies (18 percent) participating in the survey. In 132 of the companies (30 percent), a direct-giving program coexisted with a company foundation. The smaller the size of the contributions program, the more likely it is that there will only be the direct mechanism. In companies with the smallest budgets, 64 percent have this single mechanism, but this is true for only 37 percent of those with the largest budgets. On the other hand, when a company foundation is the *only* giving mechanism, companies with smaller budgets are slightly more likely to use this mechanism than are those with the largest budgets.

A dual mechanism is most prevalent in companies with larger budgets. (See Table 1.) One reason for using both is that there is a legal restriction against "self-dealing" by foundations. If there is a possibility that the company might receive some direct benefit from making a donation (e.g., discount tickets for employees), the contribution is usually made through the direct-giving mechanism.

Company foundations are set up as separate entities, although those involved in the foundation may have other corporate responsibilities (see Chapter 3). Those involved in direct programs usually report to, or have responsibility for, a specific corporate department. Which department can vary considerably.

In companies with the smallest budgets, responsibility for administration of the direct-giving program may rest with any one of several departments, including public affairs, the office of the chief executive officer, the corporate secretary, corporate administration, and person-

---

[4]For additional information on how companies organize their community affairs programs, see Nathan Weber and Leonard Lund, *Corporations in the Community*. The Conference Board, Research Bulletin No. 103, 1981.

Table 1: Corporate Giving Mechanisms (by Size of Total Contributions Budget)

Budget Size	Number of Companies	Corporate Foundation Only Number	Corporate Foundation Only Percent	Direct-Giving Program Only Number	Direct-Giving Program Only Percent	Both Mechanisms Number	Both Mechanisms Percent
$500,000 or less	209	37	18%	135	64%	37	18%
$501,000 to $1 million	98	18	18	48	49	32	33
$1.1 million to $5 million	100	19	19	32	32	49	49
$5.1 million and over	27	3	11	10	37	14	52
Total	434	77	18	225	52	132	30

nel. In general, the larger budgets become, the greater the likelihood that the direct-giving program will be administered from the public affairs or community relations area. About 30 percent of the companies with the smallest budgets have this arrangement compared to 60 percent of those in the two middle budget ranges shown on Table 2. The proportion drops to about 50 percent in companies with the largest budgets. The chief executive's office, corporate finance, corporate administration, and the corporate secretary's office are alternative choices for about a third of each budget group.

Decision Making and Governance in a Direct-Giving Program

Direct-giving programs may be governed by a contributions committee or by the company's chief executive officer, either alone or in concert with other managers. (See box, page 11.) In about 70 percent of the 357 companies that had a direct-giving program, a *contributions committee* system was used.

In the remaining 110 cases, the CEO played a prominent role, making decisions alone in about a quarter of the companies, and in consultation with the corporate board of directors in another 23 companies. For 33 of the companies, decision-making and approval authority rested with one or two senior executives, one of whom might be the CEO. In another 20 cases, approvals rested with divisional executives. Decisions in the remaining cases came from the public affairs officer, a public affairs committee, or the foundation board acting as a contributions committee.

The Contributions Committee

Membership on contributions committees ranges from two to twenty-five people, with a median of five. Companies with larger budgets appear to have slightly larger committees than do those with the smallest budgets, and the nonmanufacturing firms represented in this survey (financial institutions in particular) had slightly larger committees than did manufacturing firms. Heavy manufacturing industries, such as primary and fabricated metals and transportation equipment, have smaller committees (three to four members) than the group as a whole. Industries such as food, beverage and tobacco, printing and publishing, and merchandising are above the group median. (See Tables 3 and 4.)

In over 80 percent of the 247 cases reported, committees were management committees, while 10 percent were drawn from the corporate board of directors. The remainder were drawn from a variety of other constituencies, such as supervisory personnel and divisional executives. Departments such as public affairs, finance and human resources appeared to have the heaviest representation on committees and the person participating most often was a vice president. Divisional vice presidents also had prominent representation. (See Table 5).

In addition to the upper level managers represented in Table 5, respondents were asked if their contributions

Table 2: Organizational Location of Direct Corporate Giving Program (by Size of Total Contributions Budget)

Budget Size	Number of Companies	Public Affairs	Community Relations	CEO	Corporate Secretary	Administration	Finance/Treasurer	Personnel	Other
				Percentage Distribution[1]					
$500,000 or less	172	30%	2%	16%	15%	12%	8%	9%	8%
$501,000 to $1 million	80	41	18	7	6	7	9	4	7
$1.1 million to $5 million	81	52	7	5	11	7	7	5	7
$5.1 million and over	24	48	0	13	4	9	9	0	17
Total	357	39	6	11	12	10	8	6	8

[1]Some rows do not add to 100 percent because of rounding.

Table 3: The Corporate Contributions Committee (by Size of Total Contributions Budget)

Budget Size	Number of Companies with Direct-Giving Mechanism	Percent Having Contributions Committee	Number of Committee Members Median	Range
$500,000 or less	172	59	4	2—13
$501,000 to $1 million	80	78	6	2—16
$1.1 million to $5 million	81	84	6	2—25
$5.1 million and over	24	63	6	3—10
Total	357	69	5	2—25

Table 4: Number of Members on Corporate Contributions Committee (by Industry Class)

Industrial Classification	Number of Companies[1]	Community Size Median	Range
Chemicals and pharmaceuticals	27	5	2—16
Electrical machinery and equipment	13	5	2—8
Fabricated metal products	8	3	2—11
Food, beverage and tobacco	19	6	3—14
Machinery, nonelectrical	17	4	3—10
Paper and like products	6	6	3—7
Petroleum and gas	11	5	2—25
Primary metal industries	10	4	3—7
Printing and publishing	8	6	2—7
Stone, clay and glass products	5	6	4—7
Transportation equipment	10	4	3—5
Other manufacturing	8	4	3—5
Total: Manufacturing	142	5	2—25
Banking and finance	26	7	4—16
Insurance	23	5	3—10
Merchandising	10	6	4—8
Utilities	23	4	2—11
Other nonmanufacturing	13	4	3—10
Total: Nonmanufacturing	95	6	2—16
Total: All companies	237	5	2—25

[1] Although 247 companies reported having committees, only 237 supplied data about committee size.

committee included members below the middle-management level. Thirty-five companies indicated that they had at least one member below middle-management level (one had six). A few companies (17) also included members from outside the corporation. The median number of outsiders was three.

A small group of companies (about 15 percent) rotate the membership on their contributions committees, most typically on a biennial basis. However, rotation periods may be as frequent as one year or as infrequent as seven years. This kind of rotation is sometimes used as a method for exposing senior executives, or those who are considered candidates for the "fast track," to community and related social policy issues.[5]

[5] Seymour Lusterman, *Managerial Competence: The Public Affairs Aspects*. The Conference Board, Report No. 805, 1981.

Governance in Foundation Boards

Key decisions in company foundations are made by a board of trustees. The board may have as few as two members. Since in some cases, these two are the corporate CEO and another senior executive, the decision-making apparatus may differ little from that in the direct-giving mechanism just described. The foundation board may, however, have eight, ten or even twenty members, and their backgrounds may differ substantially from those of contributions committee members.

The Board of Trustees

The median boards of trustees of the 210 companies reporting had six members, with a range similar to that of contributions committees—two to twenty-four members. The size of the board tends to increase with the size of the

Table 5: Membership of Contributions Committees and Foundation Boards

Titles	Contributions Committee Members of Corporate Management Number	Percent[1]	Foundation Board Inside Directors Number	Percent[1]
Chairman	62	5%	108	15%
President	77	7	104	14
Vice chairman	24	2	31	4
Board members	25	2	9	1
Executive vice president	73	6	83	11
Senior vice president	34	3	62	8
Finance-Treasury				
Vice president	113	10	55	8
Other executives	50	4	9	1
Public Affairs				
Vice president	136	12	25	3
Other executives	65	6	15	2
Human Resources				
Vice president	68	6	20	3
Other executives	22	2	8	1
Administration-Planning				
Vice president	44	4	18	3
Other executives	10	1	2	—
Legal				
Vice president	36	3	10	1
Other executives	12	1	9	1
Marketing				
Vice president	25	2	—	—
Other executives	9	1	—	—
Corporate Secretary	40	3	18	3
Divisions				
President	—	—	32	4
Vice president	67	6	16	2
Other executives	16	1	2	—
Vice president (unspecified)	75	6	78	11
Other executives	50	4	18	3
All others	29	2	—	—
TOTAL	1162	100%	736	100%

[1] Percentages do not add to 100 percent because of rounding.

---

total budget. (See Table 6.) The petroleum and gas and banking and finance industries have the highest medians (8 members and 7 members, respectively), while the primary metal industries and "other manufacturing" are on the low end of the spectrum (5 and 4 members, respectively). (See Table 7.)

Foundation boards are more likely to include outside participants than are contributions committees. While only 7 percent of the committees include outsiders, about a third (67) of the foundation boards do so. Companies in manufacturing industries appeared more likely to have outsiders—their median was three outside members. Nonmanufacturers had a median of two outsiders. The range of outsiders extended from one to eighteen (see Table 7).

There also appears to be more high-level executive involvement in foundation boards. Examining foundation board membership, an executive at the level of senior vice president or above was mentioned in 53 percent of the cases, while this was true in only 24 percent of the cases with contributions committees. (See Table 5.)

Table 6: Number of Members on Foundation Boards (by Size of Total Contributions Budget)

Budget Size	Number of Companies	Number of Trustees Median	Range
$500,000 or less	69	5	2—16
$501,000 to $1 million	46	5	3—13
$1.1 million to $5 million	61	6	3—24
$5 million and over	19	9	3—14
Total	195	6	2—24

The Corporate Chairman or President as Contributions Officer

Many corporate contributions programs had their origins in the personal philanthropy of families in closely held companies. The company, through its top officer, made local contributions to organizations that might benefit its employees. Or, in some cases, it made them because a refusal to respond to certain appeals would be embarrassing to the company. The family gave to charities in which its members took a personal interest.

Critics of this style of philanthropy point out that the dividing line between personal and corporate interest sometimes becomes fuzzy. Whatever the merits or demerits of this centralized model are, it remains the one in use in many corporations with small contributions budgets. There are a number of modifications, such as the use of a committee system, and the top corporate executive in some cases is no longer a family member but a professional manager.

Among the companies surveyed for this study, 11 chairmen or presidents indicated that they were the top contributions officer. All but one of their companies had sales under $500 million, and three (nonmanufacturing) were under $100 million. All had contributions budgets of under $500,000.

As might be expected, all of these top executives reported spending less than a quarter of their time on contributions. Seven of the eleven worked through a direct-giving program and had no contributions committee. One had a committee and three had a foundation board. Eight said that they exercised discretionary authority to approve grants and were responsible for contributions policy and strategy. Seven said they screened and investigated grant requests, but six delegated related payment procedures and record keeping.

Since total expenditures were modest, few prepared formal contributions plans or budgets. No extensive efforts were made to coordinate contributions activities at field locations, although four indicated that they tried to enforce guidelines, and three indicated they provided consultation. Employee communications on contributions were developed in two of the companies, and one of these also developed contributions press releases and a public report.

Table 7: Number of Members on Foundation Boards (by Industry Class)

Industrial Classification	Number of Companies Responding	Total Membership Median	Total Membership Range	Members From Outside Corporation Number of Companies	Members From Outside Corporation Median	Members From Outside Corporation Range
Chemicals and pharmaceuticals	24	7	3—15	6	4	1—12
Electrical machinery and equipment	14	7	3—12	4	3	1—9
Fabricated metal products	13	6	3—16	6	3	1—10
Food, beverage and tobacco	16	6	3—13	5	4	1—5
Machinery, nonelectrical	17	5	3—12	6	3	1—4
Paper and like products	12	6	3—12	7	1	1—6
Petroleum and gas	9	8	3—12	5	3	1—8
Primary metal industries	14	5	3—14	5	8	3—11
Printing and publishing	5	6	3—13	2	a	3—9
Stone, clay and glass products	7	5	3—12	2	a	3—3
Transportation equipment	7	7	3—12	2	a	2—2
Other manufacturing	9	4	3—15	4	3	2—10
Total: Manufacturing	147	6	3—16	54	3	1—12
Banking and finance	16	7	3—16	1	a	2
Insurance	18	5	2—10	7	3	1—4
Merchandising	5	6	5—10	—	—	—
Utilities	2	a	3—11	1	a	8
Other nonmanufacturing	8	6	3—24	4	4	1—18
Total: Nonmanufacturing	49	5	2—24	13	2	1—18
Total: All companies	196	6	2—24	67	3	1—18

[a]For groups with two cases or less, only the range is given.

In at least 80 percent of the companies with foundations, some foundation board members were also members of the corporate board of directors. The median was two directors, whether they were insiders or outsiders, although twenty-one companies had more than five inside directors and eleven companies had six or more outside directors. (See Table 8.)

Among those most often cited as inside members of the board are the corporate chairman, the corporate president, and executive or senior vice presidents. Of the functional areas of the corporation, finance, public affairs, and human resources are most frequently represented on the boards. Executives with a rank of vice president or above are mentioned in 88 percent of the cases.

Outsiders on the foundation board are most often from a corporate, academic, legal or financial background. Titles include president, legal counsel, consultant, university department head, and the like. Almost a quarter of those mentioned were retired executives. (See Table 9.)

Both contributions committees and foundation boards usually meet quarterly, although individual companies gave frequency schedules extending the full gamut from zero to 52 times per year. If a subgroup of the committee or board exists, it typically meets about six times a year between regular meetings. Contacts among members are maintained by about two-thirds of the group on a weekly or monthly basis, most often through phone calls and written correspondence. Other methods for keeping in touch include personal contacts, circulation of meeting minutes, and scheduling site visits to agencies that are candidates for a grant.

Table 8: Members of Foundation Boards Who Are Also Corporate Directors (by Total Number of Corporate Directors Serving on Foundation Board)

Number of Directors	Inside Directors	Outside Directors
1	31	16
2	61	9
3	30	13
4	15	7
5	11	0
6 or more	10	11
Total	158	56

Number of Companies Having

Table 9: Outside Directors of Company Foundation (by Affiliation and Title)

Principal Affiliation	Number of Mentions	Percent of Total[1]
Corporate: Manufacturing	77	40%
Corporate: Service (includes banking)	39	20
Legal	18	9
Financial (excluding banking)	15	8
University and Academic	20	10
Consulting	7	4
Nonprofit	6	3
Journalism	5	3
Other	4	2
Total	191[a]	100%

Titles		
President (corporate and noncorporate)	70	37%
Retired executive	45	24
Same corporation (21)		
Other corporation (24)		
Current corporate executive (i.e. vice president, director, manager)	30	16
Lawyer	15	8
University professor or department head	10	5
Consultant	7	4
Investor	6	3
Other	6	3
Total	189[a]	100%

[1]Percentages may not total 100 percent because of rounding.
[a]Totals do not agree because some respondents did not provide both sets of information.

Chapter 3
Responsibilities of the Corporate Contributions Officer

WHEN the corporate CEO is the only corporate contributions officer, the responsibilities are limited to a few key tasks, as described in the box on page 11. Corporate chairmen or presidents may be unable or unwilling to accept primary responsibility for contributions. They may lack the time, may feel temperamentally unsuited, or as the budget grows, the function may demand a full- or part-time obligation and the development of greater expertise in making grants.

When the responsibilities are delegated below the presidential level, survey response indicates that a vice president is chosen to take charge in about 40 percent of the cases; a director or manager in about a third; a staff level person in about 10 percent. The president had responsibility in about 5 percent of the cases, and corporate officers—secretary, treasurer and so on—in the remainder. (See Tables 12 and 15.) Few of those at the vice presidential level spend more than half their time on contributions. Many said that these responsibilities took less than a quarter of their time; some delegated the more time-consuming tasks to members of their staffs.

An Overview: Reporting Relationships and Staffing Patterns

Most of those who responded to survey questions about staff size and composition had at least one staff member working on contributions. As shown in Table 10, about a quarter of the direct-giving and foundation programs had four or more staff members. However, there was a 30 percent non-response among those with direct-giving programs and a 16 percent non-response among those with foundation programs. It is likely that many of these had no "staff" in the formal sense.

Direct-Giving Programs

Professional-level staff size in direct-giving programs for the two hundred and thirty-three companies reporting ranged from one to twelve people, with one professional

Table 10: Total Staff Size in Foundation and Direct-Giving Programs

Total Staff Size	Direct Giving Number of Companies	Percent	Foundation Number of Companies	Percent
No staff, but some part-time help	23	10%	20	16%
1 staff member	48	21	16	13
2-3 staff members	108	46	54	43
4-5 staff members	28	12	13	10
6-7 staff members	14	6	12	9
More than 7 staff members	12	5	12	9
Total:	233	100%	127	100%

the median. The range of staff size for nonprofessionals (e.g., secretaries, clerks) was one to six, with a median of one nonprofessional. The data in Table 10 show an overall median staff size of almost three—the result of combining the professional and nonprofessional groups.

The figures in Table 11 indicate how staff is allocated by function as staff size grows. As might be expected, openings for specialists such as program officers and analysts grow more quickly than do those for general administrators. Secretarial staff numbers increase from one to three as staff size grows, while clerical staff goes no higher than 2 members.

The *highest* level of responsibility for the direct-giving program is placed with an employee with a contributions (or foundation) title in 49 (16 percent) of the 303 cases reporting, with a corporate executive at the level of vice president or above in 145 instances (48 percent), and with a corporate manager or other executive in about a quarter

Table 11: Median Number of Staff in Direct-Giving Programs (by Position Title)

	Position Title				
Total Staff Size	General Administrators	Program Officers	Analysts or Researchers	Secretaries	Clerks
No staff, but some part-time help	1	—	—	—	—
1 staff member	1	a	—	1	1
2-3 staff members	1	1	1	1	1
4-5 staff members	1	1	b	1	2
6-7 staff members	2	2	2	2	1
More than 7 staff members	2	2	2	3	2
Total	1	b	1	1	1

[a] Less than one full person
[b] Between one and two people

of the cases. Staff level employees such as an assistant to the president or a public affairs specialist, account for the remaining 10 percent of the cases. Reporting relationships are high: Forty-five percent report to the corporate CEO or Board of Directors; 38 percent report to a corporate vice president (see Table 12).

The backgrounds of those staffing direct programs are varied. Almost a third have a management, financial or administrative background, and about a quarter have a public affairs or communications background. Experience in program-related areas such as health, social services, education, and so on, was mentioned by 17 percent of those responding. (See Table 13.)

Company Foundations

Foundations in the survey reported professional staff sizes ranging from one to eight people, with a median of two. Nonprofessional staff sizes ranged from one to six, with a median of one. The overall staff size median is about two-and-a-half (see Table 10). The more staff there is, the more specialized the functions become. In those foundations with only part-time help, or only one staff member, that person is likely to be a secretary. Those companies with the largest staffs have medians of more than one person in each of the job categories shown on Table 14. For those companies that have both a foundation and direct-giving mechanism, there is a good deal of sharing of personnel: 46 percent of the professionals and 38 percent of the nonprofessionals had responsibilities in both programs.

Just over 100 companies responded to the question asking for the title of the highest ranking full-time foundation staff member. The results are tabulated below.

Title	Number	Percent[1]
President	29	27%
Vice President	24	22
Executive Director	22	20
Director	7	6
Secretary or Treasurer	14	13
Other	12	11
	108	100%

[1] Percentages do not add to 100 because of rounding.

Table 12: Reporting Relationships of Top Executives Responsible for Direct-Giving Program

		Number Reporting to:				
Title of Person Most Responsible for Direct-Giving Program	Total	Corporate CEO or Board	Corporate Vice President	Corporate Executive	Foundation President or Vice President	All Others
Foundation president or vice president	2	—	2	—	—	—
Foundation executive or staff	6	—	3	—	2	1
Contributions executive	30	2	15	11	1	1
Contributions staff	10	—	5	3	1	1
Corporate CEO or board	18	18	—	—	—	—
Corporate vice president	127	88	36	—	—	3
Corporate executive	76	16	47	11	—	2
Corporate staff	10	1	3	5	—	1
Others	23	14	6	2	—	1
Total	302	139	117	32	4	10

Table 13: Disciplines or Areas of Specialization among Professional Staff

Disciplines	Direct Staff (422 mentions)[1] Percent	Foundation Staff (236 mentions) Percent
Business, management administration	17%	15%
Accounting or finance	12	12
Technical (e.g., engineering)	2	5
Legal	7	8
Public affairs	17	9
Communications	9	6
Community or civic	8	11
Personnel	5	4
Health	2	6
Social service	4	5
Arts or culture	4	6
Education	7	8
Academic	5	5
Total	100%	100%

[1]Percentages do not add to 100 because of rounding.

When these foundation executives also have a corporate title, it is most often in the public affairs or contributions area. Within the corporation, almost 60 percent of these high-ranking foundation people report at the level of vice president or above, while another 30 percent are equally divided between the corporate president and an executive in the public affairs area. The remaining 10 percent are widely dispersed. (See Table 15.) Since some of these respondents appear to have vice presidencies or functions as the corporate secretary or treasurer, it is unlikely that they are really working full time on foundation matters. Rather, it appears that some of the respondents checked the highest ranking person spending a portion of his or her time on foundation matters.

The backgrounds of those working in company foundations vary widely. Slightly over a quarter have a business or financial background, just over 10 percent have a background related to community or civic affairs. Together, another quarter have skills in specialized areas related to the work of donee groups—education, health, social service, and so on.

Staff size grows with budget size (Table 16). In com-

Table 14: Median Number of Staff in Foundation Programs (by Position Title)

Total Staff Size	General Administrators	Program Officers	Analysts or Researchers	Secretaries	Clerks
No staff, but some part-time help	—	—	—	1	—
1 staff member	—	—	—	1	—
2-3 staff members	1	1	—	1	1
4-5 staff members	1	1	1	1	1
6-7 staff members	2	2	1	2	1
More than 7 staff members	2	2	1	3	2
Total	1	1	1	1	1

Table 15: Highest Ranking Foundation Officials Who Also Hold Corporate Titles

Corporate Titles and Reporting Relationships

Corporate Title of Foundation Head	Total	Corporate President	Corporate Vice President	Public Affairs Executive	Other
Vice president:					
Public affairs	18	5	13	—	—
Other	10	5	5	—	—
Executive (manager, director)					
Public affairs	21	2	13	5	1
Contributions	15	1	9	5	—
Other	4	—	2	—	2
Corporate secretary or treasurer	11	1	4	—	6
Staff:					
Public affairs	4	—	3	1	—
Contributions	6	—	3	3	—
Total	89	14	52	14	9

Table 16: Contributions Staff Size (by Budget Size)

	\$500,000 or less		\$501,000 to \$1 million		\$1.1 million to \$5 million		\$5.1 million and over	
Total Staff Size	Direct Program	Foundation Program	Direct Program	Foundation Program	Direct Program	Foundation Program	Direct Program	Foundation Program
No staff, but some part-time help	11	8	5	7	6	5	1	—
1 staff member	27	4	12	7	9	5	—	—
2-3 staff members	39	12	30	13	32	28	6	1
4-5 staff members	4	—	7	—	13	10	4	3
6-7 staff members	1	1	—	1	8	2	5	8
More than 7 staff members	—	1	—	—	6	5	6	6
Total	82	26	54	28	74	55	22	18

panies with the smallest budgets, almost half have one staff member or less, while another half (47 percent) have two to three staff members. Those with budgets in the \$501,000 to \$1 million range follow this pattern in their foundation programs, but seven companies indicated that they have four to five staff members in their direct-giving program. About half of the companies with budgets in the \$1.1 to \$5 million range have two to three staff members, while about a third have four or more. In the small group of companies with the largest budgets, half the direct-giving programs and just over three-quarters of the foundation programs have six or more staff members.

In-Depth Profiles

In addition to information about the organization of their contributions programs, the 435 companies participating in the survey were asked to complete a personal and job-responsibility profile for each professional member of the contributions staff.[1] The 524 responses came from presidents, vice presidents, managers, staff coordinators, analysts and the like. Almost half the group (43 percent) spent less than a quarter of their time on contributions, while about the same number spent more than half their time on this activity. (See chart, page 18.)

A selection of possible job requirements was outlined in the responsibility profile, and the respondents indicated whether each was a primary responsibility, one which was supervised or delegated, one for which they shared responsibility as a staff member, or not a part of their job. (See box for guidelines.) The responsibilities clustered in several major areas: work with the contributions committee or foundation board; contributions planning and budgeting; development of policy, strategy and procedures; grant screening, monitoring and follow-up; administration, including correspondence and record keeping; program initiation and discretionary approval authority for grants; work with field locations; and development of a communications program for contributions. (See Table A-1 in the Appendix for a complete list of job responsibilities.)

Overall, the respondents felt that their most important primary responsibility was to act as the liaison person between top management and outside groups seeking funds. Almost equally important was their work in coordinating the activities of their contributions committee or the foundation board. Administrative and procedural duties were also high on the list of most respondents, while preparation of communications about contributions and training field locations were least likely to be part of their duties.

Corporate Vice Presidents as Contributions Officers

About 20 percent of those returning contributions responsibility profiles were corporate vice presidents (ten senior and six executive vice presidents were also included in this category.)

About three-quarters of them report to the company president; the remainder to a vice president. Almost all (90 percent) worked with a contributions committee or foundation board. Few spent more than half of their time on contributions and 55 percent supervised contributions staff, most of them delegating such responsibilities as contributions record keeping. Over 40 percent also delegated related correspondence and payment procedures. However, 50 to 64 percent claimed primary responsibility in a number of key areas: They scheduled, prepared the agenda, and presented recommendations at

text continued on page 20

---

[1] Compensation and career path information for this group has been reported in Anne Klepper, *The Corporate Contributions Professional*. The Conference Board, Research Bulletin No. 109, 1981.

Responsibility Profile

Guidelines

Primary Responsibility: Person has sole accountability; does not share or delegate it.
Shared Responsibility: Accountability is shared:
  Supervisory   (a) by a supervisor with a staff member.
  Staff   (b) by a staff member with a supervisor.
Delegated Responsibility: Person delegates responsibility, holding another staff member fully accountable.
No responsibility: Not part of a person's job.

Functions listed most often as primary responsibilities:[1]	Percent with Responsibility
— Function as liaison between top management and outside groups seeking funds	52%
— Coordinate the work of contributions committee or foundation board:	
— Attend meetings	50
— Present recommendations	48
— Prepare agenda	45
— Schedule meetings	43
— Provide back-up materials	42
— Administration of contributions budget	47
— Screening and researching grant requests	46
— Supervise staff, if any	45
— Administering contributions:	
— Correspondence	44
— Payment procedures	41
— Developing overall contributions procedures	41

Functions listed most often as supervisory or delegated responsibilities:

— Contributions record keeping	45
— Administration of contributions payment procedures	38
— Administration of contributions correspondence	34
— Development of employee communications	29
— Screening and researching of grant requests	28
— Contributions budget administration	27
— Research and preparation of back-up materials for committee or board meetings	27
— Follow-up, monitoring, evaluation of grants	26
— Preparation of annual program budget	24

Functions listed most often as shared, staff-level responsibilities:

— Development of contributions:	
— Policy	39
— Strategy	39
— Procedures	33
— Initiation of new grant programs or projects in areas of special need or corporate interest	30
— Preparation of program budget	30
— Preparation of annual plan for contributions	28
— Functioning as liaison between top management and outside groups	27
— Evaluating overall management of function	25

Functions listed most often as outside area of responsibility:

— Contracting for use of inside or outside researchers and consultants	60
— Developing a public report on contributions	50
— Providing contributions training at field locations	51
— Developing press releases on contributions topics	51
— Preparation and administration of dues and memberships budgets	45
— Exercise of discretionary authority for grant approval	45
— Developing employee communications on contributions	37
— Monitoring field locations' contributions budgets	30
— Enforcing guidelines at field locations	28
— Scheduling meetings for contributions committee or foundation board	25

[1]Since many people handle the function alone, greater numbers listed most responsibilities as primary. The 40 percent mark was selected as an appropriate cutoff for inclusion in this summary. In the non-primary categories, 25 percent response was used as a cutoff.

RESPONSIBILITIES OF THE CORPORATE CONTRIBUTIONS OFFICER

Chart 1:
Contributions Practitioners: Salary Level, Reporting Relationship and Time Spent on Contributions

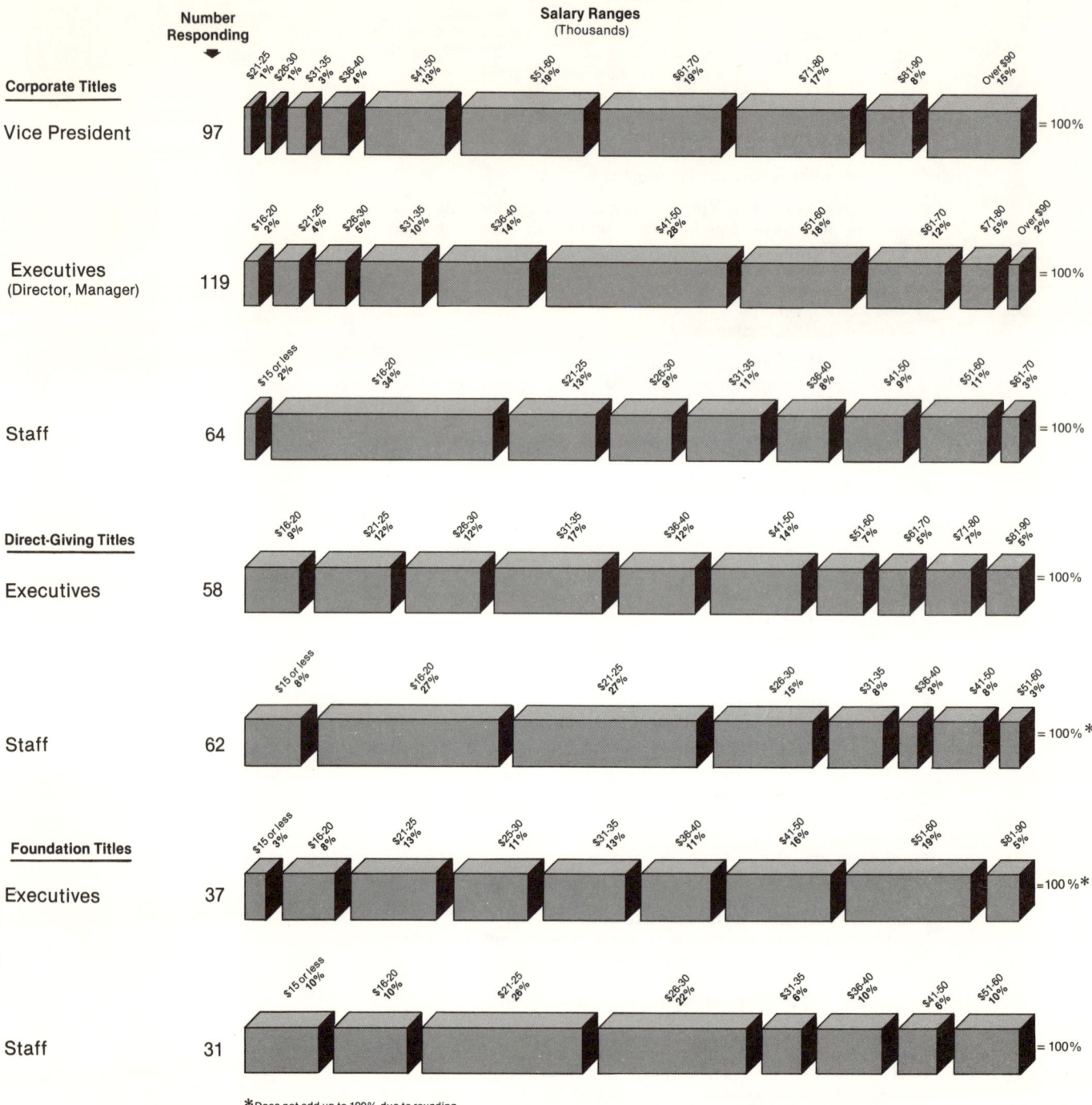

*Does not add up to 100% due to rounding.

18 THE CORPORATE CONTRIBUTIONS FUNCTION

Reporting Relationship

Corporate	Number Responding
Vice President	104

- a. 73%
- b. 27%

	Number Responding
Executives	126

- a. 22%
- b. 65%
- c. 12%
- h. 1%

	Number Responding
Staff	66

- a. 17%
- b. 34%
- c. 43%
- h. 6%

Direct-Giving

	Number Responding
Executives	61

- b. 50%
- c. 28%
- d. 12%
- h. 10%

	Number Responding
Staff	63

- b. 18%
- c. 16%
- d. 45%
- g. 5%
- h. 16%

Foundation

	Number Responding
Executives	37

- a. 16%
- b. 22%
- c. 11%
- e. 32%
- f. 14%
- g. 5%

	Number Responding
Staff	32

- c. 6%
- e. 25%
- f. 6%
- g. 53%
- h. 10%

a. Corporate President
b. Corporate Vice President
c. Corporate Executive
d. Direct-Giving Executive
e. Foundation President or Board
f. Foundation Vice President
g. Foundation Executive
h. Others▲

▲ Usually employees with staff-level titles, such as Assistant to the President.

Time Spent on Contributions

Corporate	Number Responding
Vice President	104

- a. 86%
- b. 9%
- c. 2%
- d. 3%

	Number Responding
Executives	126

- a. 70%
- b. 18%
- c. 8%
- d. 4%

	Number Responding
Staff	66

- a. 44%
- b. 35%
- c. 18%
- d. 3%

Direct-Giving

	Number Responding
Executives	61

- a. 5%
- b. 6%
- c. 26%
- d. 63%

	Number Responding
Staff	63

- a. 3%
- b. 8%
- c. 5%
- d. 84%

Foundation

	Number Responding
Executives*	37

- a. 3%
- b. 10%
- c. 10%
- d. 76%

	Number Responding
Staff	32

- b. 3%
- c. 9%
- d. 88%

a. 25 Percent or less
b. 26-50 Percent
c. 51-75 Percent
d. 76-100 Percent

*Does not add up to 100% due to rounding.

RESPONSIBILITIES OF THE CORPORATE CONTRIBUTIONS OFFICER

contributions committee or foundation board meetings. They developed the contributions policy, strategy and procedures, and prepared the annual business plan for contributions. Many (over 40 percent) also exercised discretionary authority over grants, initiated new grant programs, and prepared the annual program budget. However, preparation and administration of the budget is a task that is delegated by at least a third of the respondents.

The screening and researching of grant requests is a task often thought to be a staff function, but at least half of the vice presidents considered it a primary responsibility. Another 10 percent considered it to be a responsibility they shared as a staff member of their committee or board. Almost 40 percent delegated this responsibility.

Work with field locations was not a responsibility for almost 30 percent of the respondents, while another 30 to 40 percent considered it a primary responsibility, and about a quarter delegated it. Less than 20 percent took primary responsibility for employee communications, while about 30 percent delegated it, and almost half claimed no responsibility.

Since only 64 of the 104 respondents indicated their area of vice presidential responsibility, it is impossible to make an exact count, but the areas most frequently mentioned were public affairs, public relations, community affairs or corporate communications (a total of 27 responses), followed by responsibilities in the areas of finance, treasury or as corporate secretary (a total of 21 mentions). The remainder were dispersed, but included such areas as administration, personnel or legal.

Others With Corporate Titles and Contributions Responsibilities

When contributions responsibilities are delegated to those below the vice presidential level, the individuals frequently have such executive titles as "director" or "manager." For purposes of this study, those with titles specifically related to contributions were isolated from those with titles indicating they were members of other corporate departments or functions. The latter group, totalling 192 respondents (37 percent), is the subject of this section.

Among those who are directors or managers (126), few spend more than 75 percent of their time on the function, most spend a quarter of their time or less. They see their primary responsibilities in three areas: They screen and research grant requests and prepare related correspondence; they prepare the agenda for committee or board meetings and present recommendations at the meeting; they administer the contributions budget. Just under half (46 percent) also prepare the annual contributions plan and budget and exercise discretionary approval authority, while about a quarter supervise or delegate these tasks. About a third take full responsibility for most contributions tasks, since they have no contributions staff.

A smaller group (66) had such staff titles as assistant, coordinator or specialist. Their key responsibilities included participation in the screening and researching of grant requests and preparation of the contributions policy, strategy and procedures. About half also indicated that they had *primary* responsibility for administering the contributions budget, correspondence and payment procedures. Many (39 percent) delegated related record keeping and about a quarter delegated payment procedures. Almost half (44 percent) attended committee or board meetings and had primary responsibility for preparing the agenda and back-up materials. More than a third (37 percent) also presented recommendations at the meeting.

About 70 percent of the corporate executives and staffers share some responsibility for contacts with field locations. Roughly 40 percent of the executives consider this a primary function, while about a quarter delegate it. About a quarter of those with staff titles see this as a staff function, while 30 to 40 percent see it as a primary responsibility. Neither of the groups is heavily involved in communications such as public reports or press releases. However, about half the executives had either primary or supervisory responsibility for employee communications, while about a third of the staffers share responsibility as a staff member.

Contributions Specialists

Just over 40 percent of those submitting responsibility profiles (216) had contributions-related titles. Almost all (90 percent) spent more than half time on the function and most (75 percent) were involved for 75 to 100 percent of their time. Those with company foundation titles accounted for 42 percent of the responses; the larger portion (58 percent) had titles that placed them in direct corporate-giving programs.

Full-time vice presidents in direct contributions programs are rare, although some foundation vice presidents may also wear a direct contributions hat. Involvement by corporate vice presidents in contributions follows the patterns already discussed.

Executives in Direct-Giving Programs

Supervision of contributions staff and work with the contributions committee were among the key responsibilities of direct-giving program executives. Of the 61 respondents in this category, well over 60 percent indicated involvement in these activities. In contrast, just over 50 percent of the corporate executives were involved in all aspects of committee work (including scheduling and agenda preparation), and only 47 percent supervised staff. Development and administration of the contributions budget and consultation with field locations were primary tasks for more than half of the direct-giving executives. Almost 30 percent exercised discretionary authority to approve grants, but 48 percent said they had no authority in the area. Grant record keeping and payment procedures are frequently delegated by about half the executives, and about a third delegate headquarters budget administration as well as the monitoring of budgets at field locations.

Primary responsibilities in communications centered around the preparation of a public report of contributions—about 20 percent did some work in this area, while about a quarter delegated it. Other communications responsibilities also appeared to be delegated by at least 40 percent of the respondents. With the exception of the public report, few staffers claimed much communications responsibility. It is likely that communications, when delegated, go to another area of the company (e.g., public relations, corporate communications).

Staff in Direct-Giving Programs

While at least half of the respondents with corporate staff titles claimed *primary* responsibility for administration of the contributions budget, screening grant requests, and preparation of related correspondence, this was true for only about a third of the direct-giving staff. Just under half of the staffers attended committee meetings and presented recommendations, although this was a staff rather than a primary responsibility.

Staffers saw their key *staff* responsibilities as sharing in the preparation of the annual contributions budget (66 percent), and in the development of contributions strategy (63 percent) and procedures (59 percent). Among these 63 respondents, budget administration (47 percent) and correspondence (48 percent) also demanded attention. However, over half shared in the more creative aspects of the job: screening requests and proposals, follow up and monitoring of grants, and the initiation of new grant programs. Most (67 percent) had no discretionary authority to approve grants, although five claimed primary responsibility in this area.

Company Foundation Programs

Just under 20 percent of the respondents had company foundation titles. Presidential or vice presidential titles were held by 23 percent of 91 respondents, executive titles (director, manager) by 42 percent, and staff titles (analyst, coordinator, assistant) by 35 percent. For most of these (91 percent) contributions work was a full-time job.

Foundation Presidents: While almost 90 percent of the corporate presidents exercised discretionary authority to approve grants, this was true for only half of the ten foundation presidents who responded; the rest had no authority. Their key responsibilities were in the development of policy and strategy; presentation of recommendations at foundation board meetings; initiation of new grant programs; supervision of staff; and the overall evaluation of the management of the foundation. They delegated or supervised the preparation of the agenda and back-up materials for board meetings, proposal screening and related correspondence and record keeping, budget preparation, administration and related payment procedures, work with field locations, and the preparation of communications about contributions.

Foundation Vice Presidents: There are fewer clear-cut distinctions between primary and delegated responsibilities for the group of 11 vice presidents who reported. Most have primary authority for staff supervision and for presentation of recommendations at board meetings. However, they are less likely to delegate the preparation of the agenda and back-up materials. Most develop contributions strategy and procedures as a primary task, but are split on whether they take primary responsibility for (four) or supervise (five) development of policy, initiation of new programs, and preparation of the annual plan and budget. The same split occurs on the screening of grant requests, although seven delegated related correspondence, payment procedures, and record keeping.

Responsibility to exercise discretionary authority to approve grants was also dispersed: Three claimed primary responsibility; three claimed to supervise or delegate it; one claimed to share it as a staff member; and four indicated they had no responsibility. Three were responsible for enforcing guidelines and monitoring budgets at field locations, while six provided field consultation. Involvement with contributions communications was a primary responsibility for only two of the vice presidents.

Foundation Executives: The title of director or manager was held by 37 of those who indicated that they worked for a company foundation. Over three quarters of them had primary responsibility for supervising staff, while this was true for 67 percent of their direct-giving counterparts. Both groups are about equally likely to delegate such administrative activities as correspondence, budget administration, payment procedures, and record keeping. While 64 percent of the direct-giving executives consider liaison with outside groups seeking funds as a primary responsibility, only 45 percent of the foundation executives claim this responsibility, while 26 percent delegate it.

Foundation executives are less likely than direct-giving executives to take primary responsibility for committee and board meetings: 40 to 50 percent of the foundation executives schedule the meetings and prepare the agenda (compared to over 60 percent of those in direct giving). Between 50 and 55 percent attend meetings and present recommendations (compared to 60 to 67 percent in direct giving). Almost a quarter of the foundation executives make recommendations at meetings only as a staff responsibility. Foundation executives are also less likely to participate in formulation of policy and strategy as a primary responsibility (27 to 37 percent) than are direct-giving executives (about 41 percent).

Planning and budgeting is another area in which direct-giving executives are more likely to take a primary, or at least a supervisory, role: 70 percent of the direct-giving executives have such a role in planning, compared to 52 percent of the foundation executives. In budgeting, 78 percent of the direct-giving executives have this role, compared to 69 percent of the foundation executives. However, almost half of the direct-giving executives lack discretionary authority to approve grants, while this is true for only about a third of the foundation executives.

Over 60 percent of both sets of executives are involved primarily or as supervisors in enforcing guidelines at field locations, and over 70 percent of both groups are involved in monitoring field budgets. However, over half of the direct-giving executives claimed primary responsibility for consultation with field locations, while only a third of the foundations executives do so. An additional third delegate this responsibility.

Communications activities do not rank high as primary responsibilities for foundation executives. Preparation of a public report is a primary responsibility for about a third; an additional third delegate or supervise this task. Development of employee communications and press releases, if a responsibility at all, is usually supervised or delegated.

Foundation Staff: Overall, the range of responsibilities checked by the foundation employees with staff titles follow a more predictable "staff" pattern than do those with direct-giving or corporate staff titles. NO item was checked as a *primary* responsibility by more than 20 percent of the foundation staffers, and for items such as development of policy, strategy and procedures, no staffers claimed primary responsibility. In contrast, 20 to 30 percent of the corporate staffers claimed primary responsibility in these areas.

Foundation staffers see their chief *staff* responsibilities as participation in the development of contributions procedures (74 percent), correspondence (68 percent), and the preparation of back-up materials for board meetings. Over half also said they attend meetings and make recommendations in a staff capacity. About a quarter have supervisory responsibility over payment procedures and record keeping.

Almost 60 percent participate as staffers in screening and researching requests and proposals, initiating new grant proposals and monitoring of grants to evaluate their effectiveness. Between 35 and 45 percent have staff involvement with field locations in enforcing guidelines, monitoring budgets, and providing consultation. The communications project in which they have the most active staff participation is the development of employee communications (43 percent).

Related Responsibilities

Matching gift programs and coordination of internal employee campaigns for United Way or other federated appeals are responsibilities sometimes assigned to those handling the contributions program. In companies with large contributions budgets (over $1 million), the matching-gift program is handled by the contributions officer or foundation in over 70 percent of the cases. In companies with smaller budgets, contributions or foundation employees are involved in at least one-half to one-third of the cases, with the personnel department taking over in about 20 percent of the cases, public affairs or accounting and finance in the remaining cases.

United Way campaigns, however, are more frequently handled by the personnel department. In companies with larger budgets, there is contributions or foundation involvement in about 30 percent of the cases, but this decreases to 18 percent in companies with the smallest budgets. (See Appendix, Tables A-2 and A-3.) In larger companies, contributions responsibilities are sometimes expanded to encompass a broader "corporate support" function, with matching gifts and employee campaigns forming one component. Other components include such things as coordinating related educational programs, volunteer programs, and administering the corporate dues and memberships budget.

Chapter 4
How the Contributions Process Works

WINNING VISIBILITY, either inside or outside the corporation, has not traditionally been a high priority within corporate contributions programs. However, as both budgets and external pressures grow, conversations with those in the field indicate that this low-profile stance is changing. There is a greater need to tell the contributions story and to strengthen relationships with other departments in the corporation in order to complete the process of institutionalizing the contributions function.

Planning and budgeting appear to be key elements in making the contributions process work.[1] Starting with these elements, many in contributions, especially those with larger budgets, are involving other corporate departments, as well as field locations. While not every corporation has a formal communications element in its contributions program, at least half prepare a policy statement and a set of guidelines for field locations. Many (45 percent) prepare employee communications, and about a quarter prepare a public report.

Planning

Some form of strategic planning is done at the corporate level in approximately 300 (70 percent) of the firms responding to the survey. In 40 percent of those companies, contributions is included as part of the corporate plan. There was no response to this question on 28 percent of the returns, and it is possible that some respondents did not know whether or not contributions was part of the corporate plan. Table 17 shows the relationship between corporate and contributions planning, broken down by industry class. In fabricated metal products; printing and publishing; stone, clay and glass; banking and finance; and merchandising, more than half of the firms in this obviously small sample include some contributions planning in their corporate strategic plans.

Companies with larger contributions budgets (for the most part larger companies) are more likely than those

---

[1]Kathryn Troy, *Managing Corporate Contributions*. The Conference Board, Report No. 792, 1980.

Table 17: Corporate Strategic Planning and Contributions Planning (by Industry Class)

Industrial Classification	Prepare Corporate Strategic Plan	Contributions Is Part of Corporate Plan	
Chemicals and pharmaceuticals	36	14	
Electrical machinery and equipment	21	9	
Fabricated metal products	11	6	
Food, beverage and tobacco	21	8	
Machinery, nonelectrical	30	11	
Paper and like products	11	4	
Petroleum and gas	17	5	
Primary metal industries	16	4	
Printing and publishing	7	4	
Stone, clay and glass products	10	5	
Transportation equipment	12	3	
Other manufacturing	16	7	
Total: Manufacturing	208	80	38%
Banking and finance	26	15	
Insurance	27	9	
Merchandising	12	9	
Utilities	16	7	
Other nonmanufacturing	13	2	
Total: Nonmanufacturing	94	42	45
Total: All companies	302	122	40

with smaller budgets to prepare strategic plans and to include contributions in those plans. As Table 18 shows, the relationship between corporate planning and size of the contributions budget is more pronounced than that between budget size and inclusion of contributions in the plan.

More than a quarter of the respondents indicated that they did some function-level planning for their foundation or direct-giving program. The duration of the plans varied:

Number of Companies Having Plan:

Duration	Foundation	Direct-Giving Programs
1 year	6	11
2 years	12	11
3 years	30	26
4 years	5	4
5 years	59	53
6 or more years	1	2

While these are mostly three-to-five year plans, the time span ranged from one to eight years in the case of foundations, one to ten years in the case of the direct-giving programs.

Budgeting

In almost half of the companies that require annual budget approval by their contributions committee or foundation board, review and approval is on a line-by-line basis, with a provision for contingencies. In most of the remaining cases, the review and approval process is either on a lump-sum basis by major category (e.g., health, education, arts) or on all grants above a set dollar limit (e.g., $1,000). In only about 5 percent of the cases is the approval made solely on the total dollar amount. (See box.) However, when the corporate board of directors has a role in budget approval, it is usually to approve a total budget (or a maximum) in direct-giving programs, or the total corporate gift to the foundation.

Setting Budget Guidelines

For the total sample, the most important factor considered by the survey respondents in setting an annual budget for contributions is the level of the previous year's contributions budget. Next most important are the expected level of profit and a goal based upon pretax net income. Least important is comparison with companies that are considered "peers." (See Table 19.)

For companies with budgets of all sizes, there is agreement in giving greatest weight to the size of the previous year's budget. However, the small-budget companies next consider their expected level of profit, and then the dollar level of the grant requests they are receiving. The companies with large budgets consider what level of support will be needed to achieve their program objectives, and then look at the expected profit picture. For those companies falling into the intermediate budget ranges, the next consideration is a goal based on pretax net in-

Table 18: Corporate Strategic Planning and Contributions Planning (by Budget Size)

Total Contributions Budget Size	Number of Companies Responding	Prepare Corporate Strategic Plan Number	Prepare Corporate Strategic Plan Percent	Number of Companies Responding	Include Contributions as Part of Plan Number	Include Contributions as Part of Plan Percent
$500,000 or less	198	128	65%	129	45	35%
$501,000 to $1 million	94	70	74	75	30	40
$1.1 million to $5 million	96	78	81	84	34	40
$5.1 million and over	27	25	93	24	13	54
Total	415	301	72	312	122	39

Table 19: Factors Considered in Setting Size of Total Contributions Budget (by Budget Size)

	Average Rating[1]					Comparisons	
Budget Size	Level of Budget for Previous Year	Level of Expected Profit	Dollar Goal Based on Pretax Net Income	Level of Support Necessary to Achieve Goals	Level of Grant Requests	Others in Industry	Peer Companies
$500,000 or less	4.0	3.3	2.9	2.6	3.0	2.5	2.2
$501,000 to $1 million	3.9	3.1	3.3	2.9	2.6	2.8	2.8
$1.1 million to $5 million	3.7	3.2	3.5	2.9	2.3	2.5	2.3
$5.1 million and over	3.8	3.4	3.3	3.7	2.7	2.4	2.7
Total	3.9	3.2	3.1	2.8	2.6	2.6	2.4

[1]Key:
1 = Very little weight.   3 = A moderate amount of weight.   5 = A great deal of weight.

The Role of the Foundation Board and Contributions Committee in Budget Approval

Function	Foundation Board Number	Percent	Contributions Committee Number	Percent
Approve a line-by-line budget	86	48%	131	50%
Approve dollar totals by major budget category	53	29	78	30
Approve all grants above a set dollar limit	19	11	26	10
Approve a budget total only	9	5	14	5
Other	13	7	12	5
	180	100%	261	100%

The Role of the Corporate Board of Directors in Budget Approval

Function	Foundation Programs Number	Percent	Direct-Giving Programs Number	Percent
Approve only corporate gifts to the foundation	154	87%	n.a.	—
Approve a budget total only (or a maximum)	5	3	123	48%
Approve dollar totals by major budget category	0	0	52	20
Approve a budget total and all grants above a set dollar limit	1	1	7	3
Approve a line-by-line budget	0	0	45	18
No role	13	7	25	10
Other	4	2	5	2
	177	100%	257	100%

come, followed by the expected level of profit. Respondents were asked to rate the various factors on a scale of 1 (very little weight) to 5 (a great deal of weight), but no budget group gave a factor a rating greater than four, although some individual companies did so. More than 100 companies indicated that factors such as the size of the previous year's budget (152), the level of profit expected (113) and a dollar goal based on pretax income (124) were given a great deal of weight. However, for many of the other companies, there may be other factors—perhaps qualitative—that are weighed when setting an annual budget level.

More than 60 percent (275) of the companies responding indicated that they gave some consideration to a goal based on pretax net income when setting their budget (Table 20). The current year's income was used by about 40 percent of the companies. The remaining 60 percent were about equally divided between using the previous year or a multiyear rolling average. Only 26 percent of the manufacturing firms used the previous year's income, compared to 37 percent of those in nonmanufacturing industries. However, manufacturers were more likely to use a multiyear rolling average—31 percent used this figure as a base, compared to 23 percent of the nonmanufacturers (Table 21).

Determining a Level for Uncommitted Funds

Uncommitted funds may be provided for unforeseen requests or contingencies that arise during the year, or they may be earmarked for new program initiatives to be developed during the year. Amounts left uncommitted were slightly larger when set aside for use in foundation (a median of 18 percent) than for use in direct-giving programs (a median of 15 percent). Foundations designated a median of 10 percent for new initiatives to 9 percent for contingencies.

In direct-giving programs, the balance is in the other direction. This pattern varies slightly by budget size for direct-giving programs. However, for company foundations, there is greater variation. Those with the smallest budgets set aside more for contingencies than for new initiatives. Those with the largest budgets set aside 20 percent for new initiatives. (See Table 22.)

Headquarters and Field Allocations

Relationships between headquarters and field locations vary with program structure. Foundation grants must be approved by an officer of the foundation. Some companies assign a portion of the foundation budget to field locations, solicit field recommendations, and make final

Table 20: Basis for Setting Budget Target

Budget Size	Number of Companies	Previous Year's Income	Current Year's Income	Two-Three Year Average	Average of More Than Three Years	Other
$500,000 or less	117	30%	47%	21%	1%	1%
$501,000 to $1 million	65	40	32	21	5	1
$1.1 million to $5 million	74	23	32	38	4	3
$5.1 million and over	19	16	47	31	—	5
Total	275	29	40	27	2	2

[1] Rows may not add to 100 percent because of rounding.

Table 21: Basis for Setting Budget Target Using Pretax Net Income (by Industry Class)

Industrial Classification	Number of Companies	Previous Year's Income	Current Year's Income	Two-Three Year Average	Average of More Than Three Years	Other
Chemicals and pharmaceuticals	34	9	11	14	—	—
Electrical machinery and equipment	22	4	14	4	—	—
Fabricated metal products	14	4	7	3	—	—
Food, beverage and tobacco	19	6	8	4	1	—
Machinery, nonelectrical	20	4	10	5	—	1
Paper and like products	13	5	4	2	2	—
Petroleum and gas	15	3	5	7	—	—
Primary metal industries	13	2	6	4	1	—
Printing and publishing	10	4	2	2	1	1
Stone, clay and glass products	12	5	3	4	—	—
Transportation equipment	9	1	3	3	—	2
Other manufacturing	17	5	7	5	—	—
Total: Manufacturing	198	52	80	57	5	4
Banking and finance	21	7	7	6	—	1
Insurance	16	6	1	9	—	—
Merchandising	12	6	6	—	—	—
Utilities	17	5	9	1	2	—
Other nonmanufacturing	12	5	7	—	—	—
Total: Nonmanufacturing	78	29	30	16	2	1
Total: All companies	276	81	110	73	7	5

Table 22: Percentage of Budget Left Uncommitted (Companies Grouped by Budget Size)

	Foundation Programs			Direct-Giving Programs		
Budget Size	Median Percentage Set Aside for Unanticipated Requests	Median Percentage Set Aside for New Programs	Median Percentage for Total Uncommitted Funds	Median Percentage Set Aside for Unanticipated Requests	Median Percentage Set Aside for New Programs	Median Percentage for Total Uncommitted Funds
$500,000 or less	10	7	11	10	10	16
$501,000 to $1 million	6	10	15	8	5	15
$1.1 million to $5 million	7	10	20	10	8	15
$5.1 million and over	11	20	28	10	10	21
Total	9	10	18	10	9	15

approvals at headquarters. In other company foundations, the field has no budget; although it may recommend grants, the decision-making process is highly centralized. Table 23 shows how the participants in this survey describe headquarters-field relationships in their foundation and direct-giving programs. In about half of the latter, the field plays a primary role in determining its contributions. Either the headquarters role is minimal, or it is limited to issuing guidelines.

Overall, field locations among the group surveyed spent about 20 percent of the total contributions budget, headquarters about 80 percent (or 90 percent in companies with small budgets). (See Table 24.) However, not all of this 80 percent of the budget is likely to be spent in the headquarters community. Rather, headquarters has authority over this portion of the budget, and may approve additional requests from the field. Or, it may fund programs that are national in scope. In about 37 percent of the cases, the source of the funds spent by the field is local operating revenues; corporate funds are spent by the field in 42 percent of the cases. In the remaining 21 percent of the companies surveyed, funds from both sources are combined. When sources are combined, the field may contribute as little as 1 percent or as much as 99 percent; the median is about 20 percent.

Banks and insurance companies spend most of their budget from the headquarters location; while in merchandising, transportation equipment, and the paper industry, there is a tendency to allow more authority for spending at the field level (Table 25).

Companies with headquarters locations in New York, New Jersey, Connecticut and Ohio appear to be a little more decentralized in the authorization of contributions spending. The median expenditure by headquarters is over 90 percent in companies with headquarters in Pennsylvania, Wisconsin, Michigan, Indiana and Massachusetts. (See Table 26.)

Approval Authority

Who has the authority to approve individual grants, and what size grants may they approve without getting further authorization? Approval authority is often spread among a variety of people, from the CEO to executives at local plant sites. The CEO was cited more frequently as a source for contributions approvals in companies with smaller budgets, while contributions management received at least a third of the mentions, regardless of budget size. Approvals by a subcommittee of the foundation board or contributions committee appeared to be

Table 23: Headquarters Role in Field Decision Making

Roles	Foundation Programs Number	Foundation Programs Percent[1]	Direct-Giving Programs Number	Direct-Giving Programs Percent[1]
Headquarters role is minimal	7	5%	78	23%
Field locations have their own budget, but operate under guidelines from headquarters	14	9	103	30
Field locations have small discretionary budget, but forward most grant requests to headquarters	83	56	135	40
Field makes recommendations only	13	9	2	—
No field budget	23	15	8	2
Other	8	5	13	4
Total	148	100%	339	100%

[1]Details do not add to 100 percent because of rounding.

Table 24: Percentage of Budget Spent by Headquarters and Field Locations (Companies Grouped by Size of Contributions Budget)

Budget Size	Number of Companies	Headquarters Median	Headquarters Range	Field Median	Field Range
$500,000 or less	199	90%	5—100%	10%	0—95%
$501,000 to $1 million	94	80	1—100	20	0—99
$1.1 million to $5 million	97	77	4—100	23	0—96
$5.1 million and over	25	80	20—100	21	0—80
Total	415	80	5—100	20	0—99

HOW THE CONTRIBUTIONS PROCESS WORKS

Table 25: Percentage of Budget Spent by Headquarters and Field Locations (Companies Grouped by Industry Class)

Industrial Classification	Number of Companies	Percentage by Headquarters Median	Range	Percentage by Field Median	Range
Chemicals and pharmaceuticals	45	75%	5—100%	25%	0—95%
Electrical machinery and equipment	28	86	5—100	14	0—95
Fabricated metal products	20	90	53—100	10	0—47
Food, beverage and tobacco	28	73	5—100	27	0—95
Machinery, nonelectrical	33	75	6—100	25	0—94
Paper and like products	18	70	16—100	30	0—84
Petroleum and gas	22	83	40—100	17	0—60
Primary metal industries	20	76	25—100	23	0—75
Printing and publishing	11	79	12—100	21	0—88
Stone, clay and glass products	16	71	20—100	29	0—80
Transportation equipment	14	61	4—100	39	0—96
Other manufacturing	20	82	10—100	18	0—90
Total: Manufacturing	275	79	4—100	21	0—96
Banking and finance	33	97	45—100	3	0—55
Insurance	39	100	24—100	0	0—76
Merchandising	14	62	25—100	38	0—75
Utilities	31	80	6—100	20	0—94
Other nonmanufacturing	24	76	1—100	24	0—99
Total: Nonmanufacturing	141	90	1—100	10	0—99
Total: All companies	416	83	1—100%	17	0—99

Table 26: Percentage of Budget Spent by Headquarters and Field Locations (by Geographic Location of Headquarters)

	Number of Companies	Percent of Total Budget Spent by Headquarters Median	Range	Percent of Total Budget Spent by Field Median	Range
New England					
Massachusetts and others	18	100%	4—100%	0%	0—96%
Connecticut	24	75	5—100	25	0—95
Mid-Atlantic					
New York	56	75	5—100	25	0—95
New Jersey	16	52	6—100	48	0—94
Pennsylvania	40	94	6—100	6	0—94
East North Central					
Ohio	35	73	10—100	27	0—80
Illinois	44	85	35—100	15	0—65
Michigan	13	80	5—100	20	0—95
Wisconsin	17	90	35—100	10	0—65
Indiana	6	96	46—100	3	0—54
West North Central					
Minnesota	20	85	33—100	15	0—67
Other	14	89	50—100	11	0—50
South					
South Atlantic and East South Central	35	85	10—100	15	0—90
West South Central	27	90	20—100	10	0—80
West					
Mountain	8	73	1—90	27	10—99
Pacific					
California	34	80	20—100	20	0—80
All Other	7	88	65—95	12	5—35

more frequent in the companies with the largest budgets, although even here it received only 8 percent of the mentions (see Table 27).

When the Chief Executive Officer has approval authority, its limit is higher in the direct-giving than in the foundation programs (a median of $10,000 as against

Table 27: Individuals and Groups Having Approval Authority

	Percentage of Total Mentions by Budget Size			
Source of Approval Authority	$500,000 or less N = 638	$501,000 to $1 million N = 345[a]	$1.1 million to $5 million N = 379[a]	$5.1 million and over N = 122
Chief executive officer	17%	14%	12%	10%
Contributions management (includes all foundation and direct-giving executives with title of manager or above)	35	33	37	36
Other senior corporate executives	13	14	12	12
Contributions committee or foundation board	16	19	19	19
A subcommittee	2	2	3	8
Divisional or regional executives	9	9	7	7
Local executives	8	8	11	8
Total	100%	100%	100%	100%

[a]Details do not add to 100 percent because of rounding.

$5,000). Conversely, in the foundation mechanism, the governing board has higher limits (a median of $25,000) than does the contributions committee in a direct-giving program (a median of $10,000). The foundation executive director and the equivalent contributions executive in a direct-giving program have equivalent limits (medians in the $2,100 to $2,500 range), while program officers in foundations have higher limits (median $1,250) than those administrators with roughly equivalent positions in a direct-giving program (median $600). (See Tables 28 and 29.)

As part of the responsibility profile, data were gathered on approval limits for budgeted and contingency items. These data were analyzed by the salary range of authorizing individuals as shown on Tables 30 and 31. Overall, there is a pattern of progression in the upper limit for grant approval as the responsible individuals' salaries increase. In many, although not in all cases, the median for these limits is higher in foundation programs than in direct-giving programs for each salary level. The general pattern of higher approval levels in foundations is probably tied to the more centralized decision-making structure. In the direct-giving programs, the levels are smaller, but authority is more widely spread over many corporate levels.

Number and Size of Grants

Grant size is also larger in foundations. The median for the largest grant made by a foundation is $30,000 in companies with the smallest budgets and $625,000 for companies with large programs. Medians for comparable direct-giving programs' largest grants range from $15,000 to $200,000. With the exception of the smallest budget category, the median for the "average" size grant shows similar patterns; only the medians for the smallest grants appear to be comparable for foundation and direct-giving programs. (See Tables 32 and 33.)

Table 28: Approval Authority in Direct-Giving Programs

Source of Approval Authority	Median	Range
Chief executive officer	$10,000	$ 100—1 million
Chief operating officer	10,000	500—1 million
Chairman or vice chairman (if not either of above)	5,750	1,000—50,000
Vice presidents		
Senior or executive	5,000	200—2 million
Finance	900	100—100,000
Others	1,000	200—15,000
Contributions Committee	10,000	500—1 million
Chairman	1,000	250—75,000
Subgroup	5,000	50—100,000
Executives (Directors, Managers)		
Public Affairs	3,100	500—20,000
Contributions	2,500	100—150,000
Program Officers (or similar administrators)	600	100—250,000
Divisions or Regions		
President	5,000	100—300,000
Vice president	1,000	100—10,000
Manager	450	100—10,000
Localities	500	10—10,000

Table 29: Approval Authority in Foundation Programs

Source of Approval Authority	Median	Range
Chief executive officer	$ 5,000	$ 500—100,000
Contributions committee or foundation board:	25,000	1,000—500,000
Chairman of foundation board	2,500	500—75,000
A Subcommittee	10,000	1,500—500,000
Foundation president	5,000	500—175,000
Foundation executive director	2,150	200—70,000
Program officer	1,250	500—55,000
Others:		
Chairman or vice chairman	8,800	1,500—25,000
Public affairs executive	9,500	1,000—9,500

HOW THE CONTRIBUTIONS PROCESS WORKS

Table 30: Approval Authority for Budgeted Items (by Salary of Authorizing Individuals)

Salaries of Authorizing Individuals	Direct-Giving Programs Number of Responses	Median Amount Authorized	Range	Foundation Programs Number of Responses	Median Amount Authorized	Range
$20,000 and under......	6	625	250—5,000	3	1,000	500—5,000
21,000 to 25,000........	8	2,500	250—10,000	7	2,900	200—$1 million
26,000 to 30,000........	7	1,500	100—10,000	6	1,250	500—10,000
31,000 to 50,000........	37	2,500	200—75,000	14	4,900	500—100,000
51,000 to 70,000........	29	5,000	200—250,000	10	2,750	500—100,000
71,000 to 90,000........	11	10,000	500—50,000	4	15,000	5,000—50,000
Over 90,000	7	1,300[a]	100—50,000	2	1,000	—

[a]These are likely to be senior level executives who administer small programs in which grants seldom exceed the $1,500 level.

Table 31: Approval Authority for Contingency Items (by Salary of Authorizing Individuals)

Salaries of Authorizing Individuals	Direct-Giving Programs Number of Responses	Median Amount Authorized	Range	Foundation Programs Number of Responses	Median Amount Authorized	Range
$20,000 and under..............	7	1,000	250—5,000	3	1,000	500—5,000
21,000 to 25,000................	7	940	100—5,000	10	1,000	200—5,000
26,000 to 30,000................	10	1,500	100—5,000	8	900	500—5,000
31,000 to 50,000................	43	1,000	50—50,000	15	2,400	200—25,000
51,000 to 70,000................	34	1,000	100—25,000	13	4,800	300—20,000
71,000 to 90,000................	16	1,150	200—25,000	7	5,000	250—25,000
Over 90,000	8	1,000	100—50,000	2	1,000	—

Table 32: Grant Size for Direct-Giving Programs (by Budget Size)

Budget Size	Largest Grant Median	Range	Average Grant Median	Range	Smallest Grant Median	Range
$500,00 or less	$ 15,000	$ 100—255,000	$ 998	$ 20—25,000	$ 99	$5—10,000
$501,000 to $1 million...	49,996	1,000—465,000	1,002	100—12,000	98	5—1,000
$1.1 million to $5 million	99,875	499—1,500,000	2,004	100—20,000	51	8—1,000
$5.1 million and over....	200,000	1,000—2,700,000	3,125	100—45,377	100	5—10,000
Total...............	30,000	100—2,700,000	1,001	20—45,377	99	5—10,000

Table 33: Grant Size for Company Foundations (by Budget Size)

Budget Size	Largest Grant Median	Range	Average Grant Median	Range	Smallest Grant Median	Range
$500,00 or less	$ 30,065	$ 4,000—300,000	$1,019	$ 250—12,000	$101	$10—1,000
$501,000 to $1 million...	60,023	5,000—500,000	2,020	100—21,000	101	10—1,000
$1.1 million to $5 million	102,000	10,000—500,000	3,370	1,000—20,000	51	10—1,000
$5.1 million and over....	625,000	100,000—1,100,000	5,250	1,000—38,300	267	50—1,000
Total...............	74,022	4,000—1,100,000	2,506	100—38,300	102	10—1,000

Overall, 219 participants indicated that they had changed the average size or number of grants they made over the past three years. The trend they report is toward more and larger grants. Of the 113 respondents with foundations, 83 percent had moved toward larger grants, only 3 percent toward smaller grants. In direct-giving programs, 68 percent increased and 8 percent decreased average grant size.

Direct-giving programs appear to be slightly more likely to hold the line or decrease the *number* of grants made. About 40 percent take this stance, in contrast to 27 percent of those with foundations. This may represent an effort within some direct-giving programs to achieve greater impact by giving a smaller number of larger grants. Some company foundations have already been following this policy and may not feel the need for change. (See Charts 2 and 3.)

Supplements to Contributions

About half (218) of the survey participants make gifts that represent investments in programs that benefit society but do not qualify as charitable contributions under the Internal Revenue code. (See Table 34.) Just about all of these companies lend personnel to nonprofit or public agencies, and 75 percent of them lend services such as printing and use of office space or equipment. Others mentioned making loans at below-market rates, sponsoring employee-involvement programs, sponsoring special benefit programs (e.g., marathons) for donee groups, and gifts of equipment as examples of activities that have a social benefit. Except for loans at below-market rates, which are more frequent among banks and insurance companies, overall manufacturing and nonmanufacturing industries varied little in the kinds of activities they mentioned in response to this question.

Fewer than 20 percent of the companies that make donations other than those deductible under the IRS

Chart 2:
Change in Size of Grants over the Last Three Years, by Budget Size

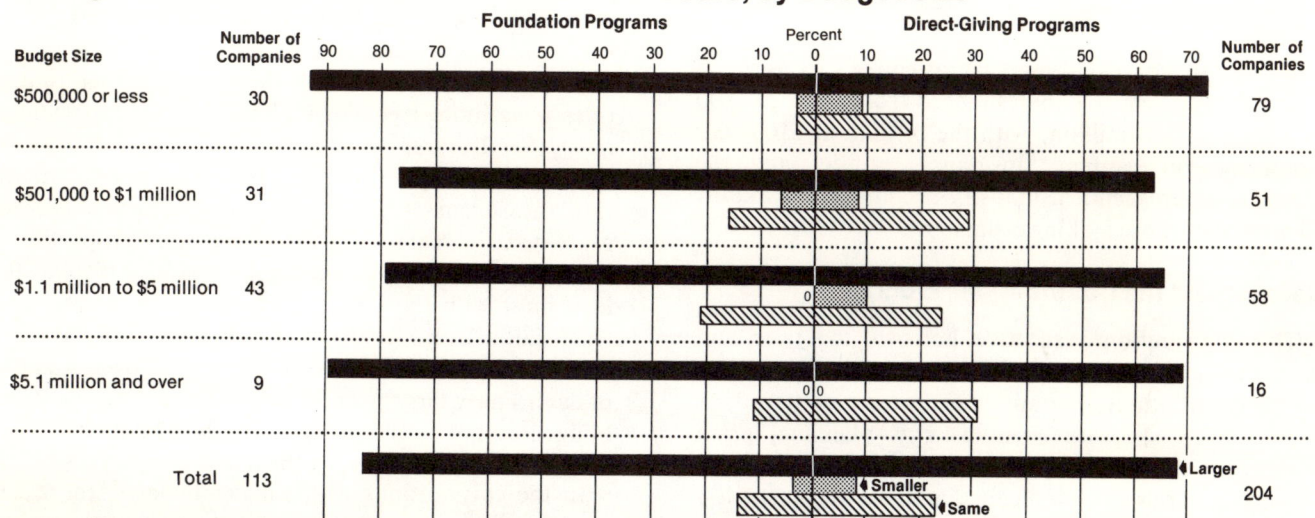

Chart 3:
Change in Number of Grants over the Last Three Years, by Budget Size

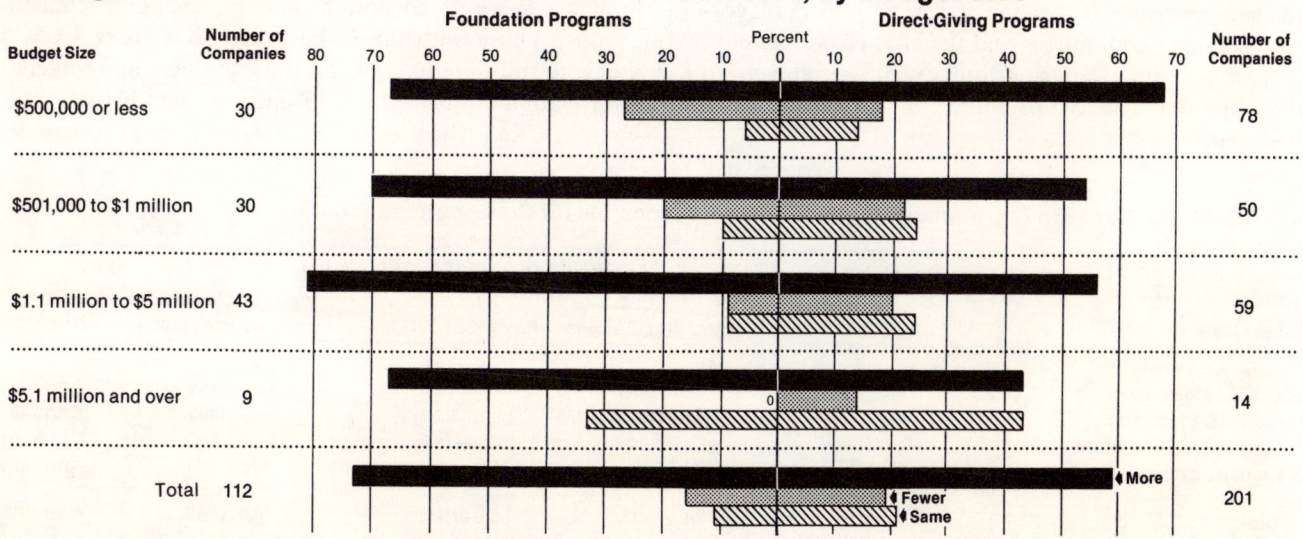

HOW THE CONTRIBUTIONS PROCESS WORKS

Table 34: Supplements to Charitable Contributions

Nature of Supplement	Manufacturing Companies Number of Mentions	Manufacturing Companies Percent of Mentions[1]	Nonmanufacturing Companies Number of Mentions	Nonmanufacturing Companies Percent of Mentions[1]
Lend personnel...	116	47%	98	49%
Lend services	94	38	70	35
Lend cash at below-market rates.......	9	4	21	10
Other.......	25	10	10	5
Total Mentions[2]...	244	100%	199	100%

[1] Details do not add to 100 percent because of rounding.
[2] There were 214 companies supplying details for this question.

definition of contributions have attempted to assign a cash value to them. Estimates ranged from a low of $400 to a high of $10 million, with the median at $100,000. Companies in banking, insurance, utilities and the chemical-pharmaceutical industry accounted for almost 70 percent of those making estimates.

Carrying Out the Contributions Program

The contributions executive borrows the time and talents of other executives and staff members for service on the contributions committee or foundation board, as well as for help with such tasks as planning, grant monitoring and evaluation, and program development. Results from this study indicate that those who spend less than half their time on the function have some advantage over their full-time counterparts. They appear to have more personal contact with influential people from other corporate departments through service with them on corporate planning committees and the like. However, both full- and part-time contributions executives appear to make extensive use of personnel in other corporate departments.

Interaction with Top Corporate Executives

Overall, the most frequent contacts between the survey respondents and a member of top management are the at least monthly interchanges with the chief executive officer. The chief financial and the chief operating officers are somewhat less frequent contacts, but there are interchanges on at least a quarterly basis. Beyond that level, contacts become less frequent: Interchanges with the executive committee of management and with the board of directors occur once a year at most.

This pattern appears to be fairly consistent throughout budget ranges. However, the companies with budgets in the range of $1.1 million to $5 million differ in that the person responsible for contributions typically meets only quarterly with the CEO, while those in the other groups meet with that executive at least monthly. While those in the other budget groups meet annually with the executive committee of management and the board of directors, those in the $1.1 million to $5 million range do not meet with them at all. (See Table 35.) There is more variation when the data are analyzed by job title, with the general pattern being one in which those with higher ranking titles have more frequent interaction with top management. (See Table 36.)

In addition to the medians for frequency of interaction, the extremes (meet monthly, do not meet at all) were examined. As Table 37 shows, a greater proportion of those in companies with the smallest budgets ($500,000 or less) meet with the CEO, chief operating officer, chief financial officer, executive committee, and board of directors than do those with budgets of over a million dollars. Fairly large proportions of those with the largest budgets do not meet at all with the chief financial officer, the executive committee, or the board of directors.

In the corporations with smaller budgets, those with responsibility for contributions are more likely to be a corporate officer, or even the CEO. As part of the top-management team, they have high-level contact routinely on a variety of corporate matters, including contributions. Those with larger budgets, while more likely to devote full time to contributions, are also more likely to have an intermediate layer of management between them and the top. These intermediaries (e.g., a Vice President

Table 35: Interaction with Top Management by Person Responsible for Contributions Program

Budget Size	Chief Executive Officer	Chief Operating Officer	Chief Financial Officer	Executive Committee of Management	Board of Directors
$500,000 or less................	Monthly	Quarterly	Quarterly	Annually	Annually
$501,000 to $1 million..........	Monthly	Quarterly	Quarterly	Annually	Annually
$1.1 million to $5 million........	Quarterly	Quarterly	Quarterly	Not at all	Not at all
$5.1 million and over...........	Monthly	Monthly	Quarterly	Annually	Annually
Total....................	Monthly	Quarterly	Quarterly	Not at all	Annually

Frequency of Interaction (medians)

THE CORPORATE CONTRIBUTIONS FUNCTION

Table 36: Interaction with Top Management by Person Responsible for Contributions Program

	Frequency of Interaction (medians)				
Titles[1]	Chief Executive Officer	Chief Operating Officer	Chief Financial Officer	Executive Committee of Management	Board of Directors
Corporation:					
Chief executive officer (5)	Does not apply	Monthly	Monthly	Quarterly	Quarterly
Vice president (102)	Monthly	Monthly	Quarterly	Annually	Annually
Executive (109)	Monthly	Monthly	Quarterly	Annually	Not at all
Staff (25)	Quarterly	Quarterly	Quarterly	Annually	Not at all
Contributions:					
Vice president or executive (33)	Monthly	Monthly	Quarterly	Annually	Not at all
Staff (16)	Annually	Annually	Biennially	Not at all	Not at all
Foundation:					
President (14)	Monthly	Monthly	Quarterly	Not at all	Annually
Vice president (9)	Monthly	Quarterly	Quarterly	Not at all	Annually
Executive (28)	Monthly	Quarterly	Quarterly	Not at all	Annually
Staff (8)	Quarterly	Biennially	Quarterly	Not at all	Annually
Total	Monthly	Quarterly	Quarterly	Not at all	Not at all

[1] Figures in parentheses are numbers of respondents.

Table 37: Interaction with Top Management by Person Responsible for Contributions Program

	Chief Executive Officer		Chief Operating Officer		Chief Financial Officer		Executive Committee of Management		Board of Directors	
Budget Size	Monthly or more	Not at All	Monthly or more	Not at All	Monthly or more	Not at All	Monthly or more	Not at All	Monthly or more	Not at All
$500,000 or less	66%	7%	48%	18%	48%	21%	21%	46%	9%	48%
$501,000 to $1 million	53	8	47	20	41	22	22	49	3	49
$1.1 million to $5 million	46	17	35	23	27	27	8	65	2	58
$5.1 million and over	52	7	52	17	23	31	9	41	—	52
Total	57	10	45	20	39	24	15	51	5	51

for Public Affairs) represent them, and, when appropriate, present their recommendations to the executive committee of management and the board of directors.

About 90 participants reported contacts with special board committees, most often a public policy or other contributions-related committee (53 percent of the cases), but also with the executive committee (18 percent), audit committee (13 percent), compensation committee, and finance committee (each about 8 percent).

Influence on Program Content and Grant Size

As might be expected, the chief executive officer and the contributions committee or foundation board appear to be more influential in decisions about grant size and program content than do other top corporate managers such as the chief financial officer, the chief operating officer, or the corporate board of directors. Using a rating scale of 1 (very little influence) to 5 (a great deal of influence), participants gave the contributions committee or foundation board a 4.4 rating for influence on both program content and grant size. In contrast, the corporate board of directors and its special committees received a 1.9 and a 1.8 rating, respectively, on program content. For grant size, the board received a 2.0 rating, while its special committees were rated 1.6. This pattern appears to hold across all budget categories, with the CEO having most influence over both grant size and program content in companies with the smallest budgets. (See Tables 38 and 39.)

Interaction with Related Corporate Departments

There are frequent contacts on contributions-related matters with public affairs, public relations and community relations departments. They most usually meet with the respondents in the range of once a month to bimonthly. Those with specific contributions titles, as well as foundation directors or managers, also meet on about this frequency with members of the personnel department. The remainder of the group meet with Per-

Table 38: Influence of Corporate Executives and Governing Groups on Program Content (by Size of Budget)

	Average Amount of Influence[1]					
Budget Size	Corporate Board of Directors	Special Committees of Board of Directors	CEO	COO	Chief Financial Officer	Contributions Committee or Foundation Board
$500,000 or less	2.1	1.6	4.1	3.0	2.5	4.3
$501,000 to $1 million	1.8	1.9	3.7	2.8	2.2	4.6
$1.1 million to $5 million	1.9	2.1	3.5	2.6	1.9	4.5
$5.1 million and over	1.9	2.3	3.5	2.8	2.0	4.3
Total	1.9	1.8	3.8	2.8	2.2	4.4

[1]Key
1 = Very little 3 = Moderate amount 5 = Great deal

Table 39: Influence of Corporate Executives and Governing Groups on Size of Grants (by Size of Budget)

	Average Amount of Influence[1]					
Budget Size	Corporate Board of Directors	Special Committees of Board of Directors	CEO	COO	Chief Financial Officer	Contributions Committee or Foundation Board
$500,000 or less	2.2	1.5	4.1	3.1	2.6	4.4
$501,000 to $1 million	2.0	1.7	3.8	2.9	2.2	4.6
$1.1 million to $5 million	1.7	1.7	3.6	2.5	2.1	4.5
$5.1 million and over	1.8	2.1	3.7	2.8	2.1	4.2
Total	2.0	1.6	3.9	2.9	2.3	4.4

[1]Key
1 = Very little 3 = Moderate amount 5 = Great deal

sonnel about three times a year. (See Table 40.) The smaller the budget, the less frequent the meetings, probably because contributions work demands a proportionately small amount of time. Other departments mentioned by respondents as frequent contacts included finance and accounting, tax and legal, and the president's office. Contacts with branch and plant locations were also mentioned.

About 30 percent of those responding served on corporate planning committees with members of the departments mentioned above. Those with corporate (non-contributions) titles are most likely to be involved; those with foundation titles, least likely. Practitioners with medium to medium-large budgets are also more likely to serve on corporate planning committees than are those with very large or small budgets. This is probably because specialized contributions personnel are in charge of the largest budgets; CEO's or other senior executives are in charge of the smallest budgets. The budget sizes in between are more often managed by employees with multiple responsibilities (e.g., corporate treasurer or secretary, public affairs officer).

Use of Other Departments for Contributions-Related Matters

Over 40 percent of those responding indicated that they used people from other departments to help in such contributions-related tasks as proposal screening (66 percent), program planning (47 percent), and monitoring and evaluation of grants (41 percent). The number of people from other departments used in this way over the course of a year varied from one to three hundred, but the median was ten. Personnel, public and community affairs, and field, group or divisional locations received the most frequent mentions in all categories. Use of other departments, such as those with research or technical expertise, varied with the nature of the task. (See Table 41.)

Paid outside consultants were used by a small number of companies. For proposal screening, 23 companies employed outsiders; 27 companies used them for program planning; and 17 companies used them for monitoring and evaluation. The number of paid assignments in a given year varied from one to fifteen, but one assignment was the median for program-planning purposes, and two

Table 40: Frequency of Interaction between Contributions Personnel and other Departments

Frequency	Public Affairs-Public Relations Number	Public Affairs-Public Relations Percent	Community Relations Number	Community Relations Percent	Personnel Number	Personnel Percent	Other[1] Number	Other[1] Percent
Once a month or more	202	62%	148	60%	139	40%	88	69%
Three to four times per year	53	16	40	16	94	27	26	20
Once or twice a year	20	6	15	6	52	15	9	7
Rarely or never	51	16	45	18	62	18	5	4
Total	326	100%	248	100%	347	100%	128	100%

[1]Includes such departments as finance, legal, tax; branch and plant locations.

Table 41: Use of Other Corporate Departments for Contributions-Related Tasks

Departments Mentioned	Proposal Screening (503)[a]	Program Planning (331)[a]	Grant Monitoring and Evaluation (276)[a]
Executive office or administration	3%	4%	5%
Field groups, divisions	11	10	8
Personnel	20	20	21
Public and community affairs	16	18	18
Finance, accounting and treasury	5	10	7
Research and technical	8	6	11
Legal and tax	9	7	6
Medical	6	4	6
Sales, marketing and consumer	7	6	9
Planning	1	1	1
Special Groups			
College Relations	2	3	2
EEO and Affirmative Action	2	1	2
"Varies with nature of grant or program"	5	10	4
Other	4	1	—
Total	100[b]	100[b]	100[b]

[a]Number in parenthesis is total response.
[b]Columns may not add to 100 percent because of rounding.

assignments the median for proposal screening, grant monitoring, and evaluation.

The larger the budget, the more likely companies were to use both insiders and outsiders for these contributions-related tasks. Only a third to a half of the companies with the smallest budgets used other departments, while over 80 percent of the companies with the largest budgets did so (see Table 42).

Communications

At least half of the survey participants prepare internal communications in the form of a contributions policy statement and guidelines for use in field locations. Almost half (48 percent) prepare employee communications. About a quarter prepare communications for the public in the form of a contributions report or press releases on individual grants. Those with the smallest budgets are less likely than are those with budgets of more than $500,000 to prepare any form of communications, except a policy statement. Companies with the largest budgets are highly likely to engage in all forms of internal and external communications. (See Table 43.)

Industry Patterns

Individual industries—such as merchandising and petroleum and gas—stand out for their heavy involve-

Table 42: Use of Other Departments and Consultants for Contributions-Related Tasks

		Other Departments			Outside Consultants		
Budget Size	Number of Companies[1]	Screen Requests	Plan Contributions Programs	Monitor/ Evaluate Grants	Screen Requests	Plan Contributions Programs	Monitor/ Evaluate Grants
$500,000 or less............	189	50%	36%	29%	3%	2%	2%
$501,000 to $1 million........	92	70	45	36	4	5	3
$1.1 million to $5 million......	100	89	60	58	8	10	4
$5.1 million and over.........	27	92	81	92	27	36	32
Total....................	408	66	47	41	6	7	4

[1]This question allowed the respondent to answer yes or no. The number of companies is the total response to the question; the percentages indicate that portion responding "yes."

Table 43: Communications Practices in Contributions Programs (by Budget Size)

Budget Size	Number of Companies	Prepare Guidelines for Field	Prepare Contributions Policy Statement	Prepare Public Report of Contributions	Prepare Press Releases	Prepare Employee Communications	Prepare Shareholder Communications
$500,000 or less.....................	196	39%	63%	9%	12%	31%	4%
$501,000 to $1 million................	94	59	71	26	26	49	13
$1.1 million to $5 million..............	95	65	79	41	49	70	17
$5.1 million and over.................	26	76	81	69	69	85	15
Total........................	411	52	69	24	28	48	10

Table 44: Communications Practices in Contributions Programs (by Industry Class)

Industrial Classification	Number of Companies	Prepare Guidelines for Field	Prepare Contributions Policy Statement	Prepare Public Report of Contributions	Prepare Press Releases	Prepare Employee Communications	Prepare Shareholder Communications
Chemicals and pharmaceuticals.......	45	64%	80%	31%	47%	67%	18%
Electrical machinery and equipment ...	29	48	48	18	24	48	10
Fabricated metal products............	19	53	74	16	16	21	5
Food, beverage and tobacco..........	27	70	74	18	22	33	15
Machinery, nonelectrical.............	37	59	70	16	11	30	5
Paper and like products	18	61	55	17	17	39	—
Petroleum and gas	21	67	81	48	52	90	19
Primary metal industries	20	40	70	25	40	55	15
Printing and publishing	12	42	50	17	25	67	—
Stone, clay and glass products	16	38	62	25	19	44	12
Transportation equipment.............	14	64	57	14	21	50	7
Other manufacturing	17	59	76	18	35	59	12
Total: Manufacturing	275	57	68	24	28	50	11
Banking and finance.................	33	42	70	51	30	48	6
Insurance.........................	39	26	72	28	36	54	13
Merchandising.....................	13	69	85	15	46	85	15
Utilities...........................	28	57	71	11	7	14	11
Other nonmanufacturing	23	43	74	9	26	35	—
Total: Nonmanufacturing............	136	43	73	26	28	44	9
Total: All companies................	411	53	70	24	28	48	10

Table 45: Companies Reporting Contributions in Annual Report

Industrial Classification	Number of Companies	Current Year	Last Five Years
Chemicals and pharmaceuticals	45	15	15
Electrical machinery and equipment	29	4	8
Fabricated metal products	19	1	2
Food, beverage and tobacco	27	6	11
Machinery, nonelectrical	37	3	7
Paper and like products	18	2	3
Petroleum and gas	21	8	10
Primary metal industries	20	5	6
Printing and publishing	12	2	4
Stone, clay and glass products	16	2	2
Transportation equipment	14	3	5
Other manufacturing	17	—	4
Total: Manufacturing	275	51	77
Banking and finance	33	11	16
Insurance	39	9	9
Merchandising	13	3	4
Utilities	28	1	1
Other nonmanufacturing	23	2	4
Total: Nonmanufacturing	136	26	34
Total: All companies	411	77	111

ment in all forms of communication. While only two of the thirteen merchandisers that responded published a public report on contributions, 85 percent prepared both a policy statement and communications for their employees. Almost 70 percent prepared field guidelines and almost half prepared press releases about contributions. Since these establishments are usually highly visible representatives of business in any community, it is not surprising that they have felt the need for a written policy statement and a desire for press recognition. Also, since merchandising companies often have many outlets that are widely dispersed geographically, the need for headquarters to issue a uniform set of field guidelines may be more critical than it is in some other industries.

About half of the petroleum and gas companies prepare a public report on their contributions, as well as press releases. This industry has received close scrutiny from government, the press, and the public. Disclosure may be one of several strategies these companies have chosen as a means for managing the situation. However, respondents in this industry are also heavily involved in internal communications, with 80 percent preparing a policy statement and 90 percent preparing communications for employees.

In industries that are under some form of government regulation, public reporting in the form of a contributions report or press releases runs the gamut from a low-profile stance in utilities (only about 10 percent involved) to a moderate stance by the insurance industry (about one-third involved) to an "up front" stance by those in banking. About a third of the banking and financial institutions prepared press releases, while half issued a public report. Many of these banks are affected by the Community Reinvestment Act, which requires disclosure of their efforts to ascertain and meet the credit needs of the residents in the communities where they operate.[2] (See Table 44.)

Shareholders

One additional group with which companies may communicate about their contributions activities is their shareholders. While only 41 companies indicated that they prepared specific shareholder communications, about 20 percent indicated that information about contributions had been included in their corporate annual reports during the current year, and 27 percent said information had been included within the past five years. (See Table 45.) In some corporations that prepare a public report, it has been a practice in the annual report to notify shareholders of its availability.

[2]Nathan Weber, *Banks, Neighborhoods and the Community Reinvestment Act.* The Conference Board, Information Bulletin No. 85, 1981.

Appendix

Job Responsibility Profile

Table A-1: Contributions Job Responsibility Profile

Description of Task	Number of Individuals Responding	Primary	Delegate or Supervise	Staff	None
Function as liaison between top management and outside groups seeking funds	514	52%	18%	27%	4%
Administer the contributions:					
Budget	515	47	27	17	9
Payment procedures	511	41	38	11	9
Correspondence	515	44	34	18	3
Record-keeping	516	37	45	10	8
Screen and research all requests for grants	514	46	28	24	2
Supervise contributions staff	471	45	13	7	35
Coordinate work of contributions committee or foundation board:					
Prepare agenda	411	45	19	16	20
Schedule meetings	474	43	20	12	25
Research and prepare back-up material	482	42	27	22	9
Attend meetings	473	50	15	21	15
Present recommendations	478	48	14	23	14
Prepare the annual:					
Business plan for contributions	490	39	18	28	16
Budget for contributions:					
Administrative budget	483	38	22	28	15
Program (grants) budget	484	38	24	30	8
Develop the overall corporate contributions:					
Policy	508	33	18	39	10
Strategy	503	35	18	39	8
Procedures	510	41	22	33	4
Evaluate overall management of contributions function	481	38	15	25	22
Initiate new grant programs or projects in areas of special need or special corporate interest	502	36	21	30	14
Coordinate contributions at field locations:					
Enforce guidelines	462	34	21	17	28
Monitor budgets	459	33	23	14	30
Provide consultation	470	39	20	19	23
Provide training	438	19	19	12	51
Coordinate follow-up, monitoring and evaluation of grant effectiveness	482	32	26	24	18
Exercise discretionary authority to approve grants	438	27	12	16	45
Responsibility for dues and memberships budget:					
Prepares budget	474	26	17	11	47
Administers budget	471	25	19	11	45
Contract use of inside/outside researchers and consultants	449	21	9	10	60
Develop and implement plan for communicating the contributions "story":					
Develop a public report	466	15	19	15	50
Develop employee communications	472	16	29	18	37
Develop press releases	464	11	26	12	51

[1] Percentages may not add to 100 percent because of rounding.

Table A-2: Company Foundation Presidents and Vice Presidents

Reporting Relationship	Foundation President	Foundation Vice President
Foundation Board[1]	2	2
Foundation President	—	3
Foundation Vice President	—	1
Corporate CEO	3	—
Corporate Vice President	3	3
Corporate Executive	1	2
Salary Level ($000)		
$16-20	—	1
21-25	—	1
26-30	—	1
31-35	1	1
36-40	—	1
41-50	1	2
51-60	—	1
61-70	2	2
71-80	4	1
81-90	1	—
Time Spent on Contributions		
25 percent or less	1	1
26-50 percent	—	—
51-75 percent	3	2
76-100 percent	6	8

[1] Technically, all foundation presidents report to the foundation board, but several respondents supplied their corporate reporting relationship.

Table A-3: Department Administering United Way Campaign (by Size of Total Contributions Budget)

Budget Size	Number of Companies	Contributions or Foundation	Personnel	Public Affairs/ Relations	Accounting/ Finance/Treasurer	Rotates	Other
		\multicolumn{6}{c}{Percentage Distribution[a]}
$500,000 or less	176	18%	55%	7%	7%	2%	10%
$501,000 to $1 million	92	23	52	13	1	4	7
$1.1 million to $5 million	98	31	41	8	3	6	11
$5.1 million and over	27	33	48	4	0	4	11

[a] Percentages may not add to 100 percent because of rounding.

Table A-4: Department Administering Matching Gifts (by Size of Total Contributions Budget)

Budget Size	Number of Companies	Contributions or Foundation	Personnel	Public Affairs/ Relations	Accounting/ Finance/Treasurer	Other
		\multicolumn{5}{c}{Percentage Distribution[a]}
$500,000 or less	109	32%	27%	14%	12%	16%
$501,000 to $1 million	76	57	17	10	10	5
$1.1 million to $5 million	89	73	13	4	6	3
$5.1 million and over	22	82	9	—	—	9

[a] Percentages may not add to 100 percent because of rounding.

APPENDIX

WITHDRAWN